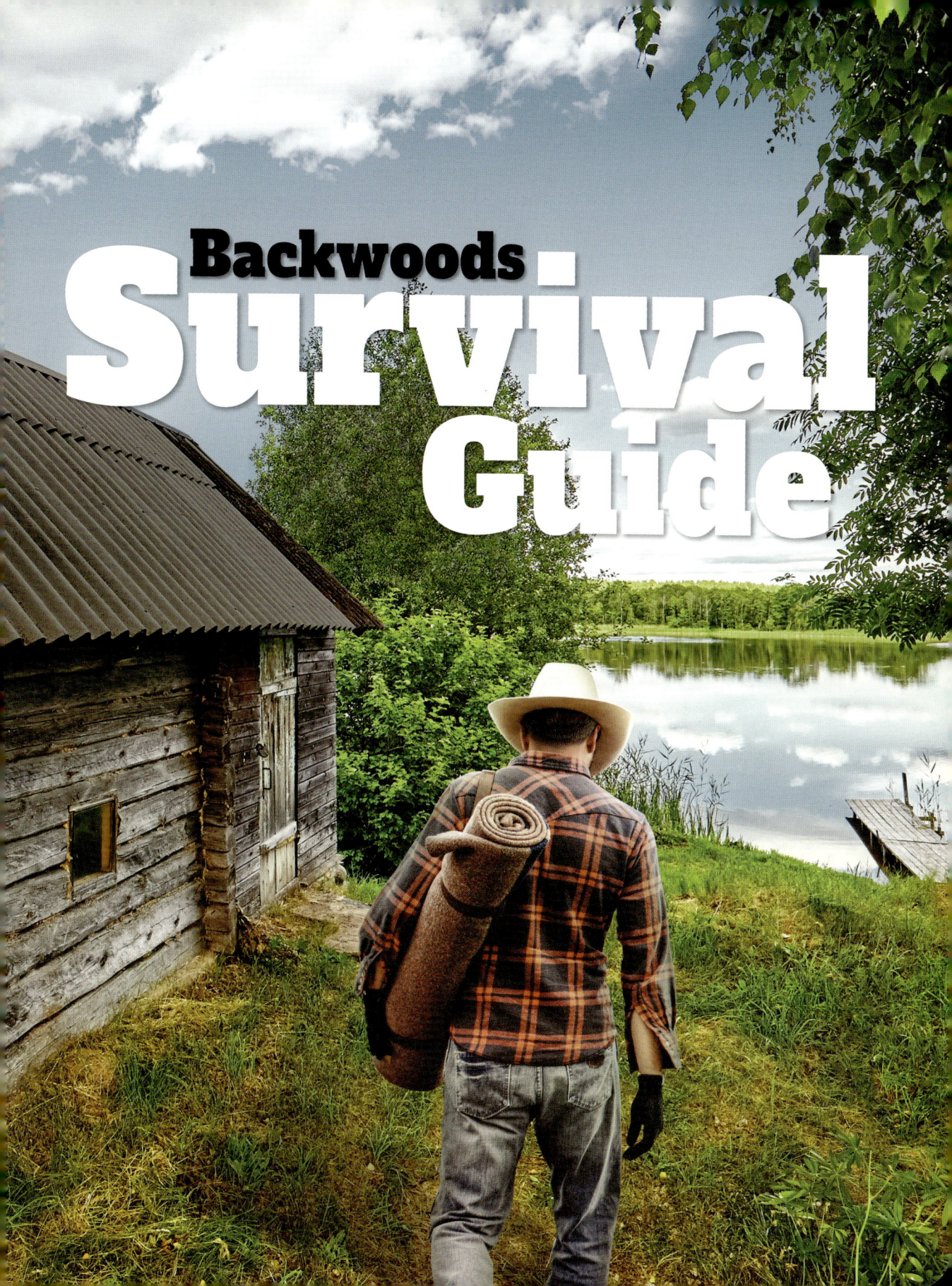

Backwoods Survival Guide

PRACTICAL ADVICE FOR THE SIMPLE LIFE

JIM COBB

CONTENTS

100

CHAPTER 1
BUSHCRAFT

12 COMMON WILD MEDICINALS

22 BENEFITS OF TRACKING

30 HOME SWEET HOME

38 WOODSY WOMEN

50 MEET THE STAFF

CHAPTER 2
HOMESTEADING

64 THE SURVIVAL GARDEN

76 HARVESTING A PRECIOUS RESOURCE

84 PLANTING THE SEED OF SELF-RELIANCE

92 PRESERVING THE HARVEST

CHAPTER 3
SURVIVAL PLANNING

102 HITTING THE TRAIL

114 BACKCOUNTRY FIRST-AID ESSENTIALS

126 SURVIVAL PSYCHOLOGY

138 BUILDING SURVIVAL

CHAPTER 4
DIY PROJECTS

148 MAKE YOUR OWN OILCLOTH TARP

156 LIGHT IT UP AND LET IT BURN

164 KNOT IMPORTANCE

176 REEL 'EM IN!

186 INDEX

64

30

INTRODUCTION

YOUR BACKWOODS SURVIVAL GUIDE

When we first started to create *Backwoods Survival Guide,* our goal was to craft a publication that would help those who wanted to pursue a self-reliant lifestyle. But, then the question became: What is self-reliance? What sorts of topics would fall under that umbrella?

We decided that we would rather err on the side of inclusion than exclusion. The fact is, there are many facets to self-reliance, including the following:

BUSHCRAFT

Being able to walk into the woods and build what you need in order to survive, from shelters to traps and more, is a key element of self-reliance. We also include in this category general wilderness survival skills such as navigation and emergency signaling.

HOMESTEADING

This includes all manner of topics and information that relate to growing and preserving food, raising animals and harvesting rainwater, and all the different ways we can work to be able to provide for our own basic needs at home.

FORAGING

This is sort of a kissing cousin to bushcraft. Having knowledge and experience in recognizing and making use of wild edibles and medicinals goes a long way toward helping you become more independent.

DIY

Being self-reliant involves having the skills and ability to make repairs, complete projects and otherwise be able to get things done with little or no outside assistance. We all start somewhere, and this is one area where most of us are constantly learning.

FINANCIAL INDEPENDENCE

While winning the lottery would be helpful, the reality is that financial know-how is within the grasp of most people—if only they would take the time to learn. Being self-reliant means being able to weather at least minor hits to the budget because you've planned ahead.

PREPAREDNESS

Whether you call it disaster readiness, prepping or survivalism, the goal is the same—being able to handle little, and maybe not so little,

INTRODUCTION

curveballs. This includes such things as putting away food and supplies for emergencies as well as stocking kits for home and vehicles.

Nobody is born knowing everything there is to know about self-reliance. For some, it comes naturally, either because of seemingly innate skills or because they are raised in an environment that fosters the knowledge and experience. Once upon a time, many, if not most, people grew up tending large gardens, harvesting wild game, raising food animals like chickens and rabbits, preserving food at home through canning, making and mending clothing, and performing any number of other chores that, when put together, meant the family could satisfy most or all of their basic needs on their own.

Today, many of those same tasks seem outdated, maybe even quaint, to a lot of people. Yet, more and more of us have a desire to get back to our roots, so to speak, and explore some of the skill sets that our grandparents or great-grandparents may have taken for granted.

For some, it is a way to save money, as quite often doing something yourself is cheaper than paying someone else to do it. For others, it is a desire to be more independent, just in case the world starts to go sideways and the luxuries we enjoy now, such as indoor running water and fresh fruit on demand, become harder to achieve.

Whatever the reason is for pursuing self-reliance, that's where this book, *Backwoods Survival Guide*, comes into play.

Here, we've gathered together some of the top experts and instructors in the self-reliance world and tasked them with sharing their knowledge and expertise. Some have contributed what has been their first published works. Others already have long-established writing careers. This book is designed to provide a well-rounded mix of topics that will appeal to anyone looking to live a more self-reliant lifestyle.

In the Bushcraft section, we're covering how to forage for wild edibles and tracking animals, so you'll be able to find things to eat when you're in the field. While you're out there, you might find it necessary to seek shelter for the night, so we've also addressed that need. And since we know it's not just the guys who are looking for more information, we've been sure to include information that will also focus on the unique needs of women.

The focus in our Homesteading section is on food and water, with information on how to plan and plant a survival garden—which might be a bit different than the traditional garden in the suburbs. Rainwater is a very precious resource, so we wanted to make sure to include an article on collecting it properly. Once you've harvested your garden, you'll want to save the seeds for next year, of course. In addition to saving seeds, you'll need to know how to preserve your harvest for the long haul.

In Survival Planning, the information centers around looking at ways to keep yourself alive when you hit the trail. We start with how to plan each trip with safety in mind, and address basic first-aid essentials, should you or one of your party get injured. One of the most important aspects of survival is mental preparation. Survival truly begins and ends between your ears, so we made sure to include a piece on survival psychology, as well as some common survival myths about water.

Finally, in our DIY section, we've chosen some of the most popular projects for readers, including how to make an oilcloth tarp and the importance of a fire kit. And no survival guide is complete without a section on how to tie and use common knots.

We truly hope you enjoy this *Backwoods Survival Guide*. We trust you will find the information in this book useful and appropriate, and a handy reference guide that you can pull out to keep your survival skills sharp no matter where you may find yourself.

Many survival skills are useful whether you're in your home or exploring the great outdoors.

YOUR TIME EXPLORING NATURE WILL BE MORE ENJOYABLE IF YOU'RE PREPARED.

CHAPTER 1
BUSHCRAFT
**ALSO KNOWN AS WILDERNESS SURVIVAL—
IT'S TIME TO GET OUTSIDE AND THRIVE.**

BUSHCRAFT

COMMON WILD MEDICINALS

Mother Nature has an entire first-aid kit out there, if you know how to find and use the right plants.

PRICKLY PEAR

WILD MINT

WILLOW TREE

GARLIC

ALOE

NETTLE

BUSHCRAFT

SOME PLANTS REQUIRE JUST A QUICK CLEANING; OTHERS SHOULD BE COOKED.

The author cleaning the glochids and spines from a cactus pad

14 BACKWOODS SURVIVAL GUIDE

HERBAL MEDICINE IS BECOMING MAINSTREAM. THAT'S WHY PEOPLE ARE ASKING QUESTIONS ABOUT THE PRESCRIPTIONS THAT DOCTORS GIVE THEM. PATIENTS ARE UNDERSTANDABLY CONCERNED ABOUT THE NEGATIVE CONSEQUENCES OF THE DRUGS THAT ARE USED TO REMEDY SPECIFIC AILMENTS. SOMETIMES THE SIDE EFFECTS SEEM AS BAD AS THE DISEASE.

A doctor friend tells me that in the past 15 years, he's been prescribing more and more herbal medicines to his patients. He revealed that he had little confidence in these herbs, but patients have been demanding them. We have had lots of discussions about the value of medicinal herbs. I have presented him with clinical data and his attitude has changed, little by little. There are drugs, for example, that have been used for diabetic patients, where the drug caused the death of the patient. At least if you are taking prickly pear for diabetes, and the prickly pear is ineffective for your condition, there are no side effects, except that you are eating cactus!

I have collected real testimonials and clinical data over the past 20-plus years, documenting that there are effective alternatives to antibiotics and other drugs so commonly used by today's doctors. These findings are compiled in my *Integral Health* book, where I also explore the ancient practices of Hippocrates in which he healed with sunlight, water therapy, diet and fasting, exercise, and other practices that supposedly became the foundation of modern medicine.

Here are a few of the commonly available medicinal plants that I've found to be effective and safe.

BUSHCRAFT

TRY THESE EASY-TO-FIND NATURAL REMEDIES

NETTLE

Nettle is a common wild plant throughout the world and it is generally a very underrated herb.

I've eaten the greens like spinach for decades, and enjoy it. But once I heard about using an infusion of the nettle leaves (dried or fresh) for allergies, I started drinking it pretty regularly in the evenings. It has helped to relieve congestion and improved my ability to breathe. It seems to work even better than my old standby, Mormon tea.

There is nearly always a rich supply of nettle greens in the spring, and property owners have always allowed me to pick the nettles growing on their land.

Michael Moore, author of *Medicinal Plants of the Mountain West*, describes nettles as a diuretic and astringent, and he advises the tea for use in cases of internal bleeding.

WILLOW

Willow trees are found in wet areas around the world. Though I often use the wood for craft projects, it's the bark that has long been used as a medicine. The inner bark of willow contains salicin and is the original aspirin. The bark of the younger shoots is strongest and it is fairly easy to harvest. When steeped in water, willow tea is good for headaches, fevers and even hay fever. Due to its strong antiseptic properties, the tea can also be used as a good mouthwash, or used externally on wounds. A willow wash is said to work wonders on rheumatism sufferers.

Willow plants are somewhat diverse in appearance. Some are small and bushy and others are tall trees. Their leaves are nearly all thin and lance-shaped. The plant is found along streams. I have seen them at sea level and higher than 8,000 feet. They are found throughout North America.

Nettle leaves

Willow bark

16 BACKWOODS SURVIVAL GUIDE

Prickly pear cactus pads are much tastier after being cooked to eliminate their interior sliminess.

KNOWING HOW TO PREPARE PLANTS AND HERBS IS AS IMPORTANT AS IDENTIFYING THEM.

Mint leaves

PRICKLY PEAR CACTUS

Generally, we use the term "prickly pear" for all of the oval-padded cacti of the Opuntia genus. They have been used for centuries in Mexico as food and medicine. The pads, once cleaned of their spines, can be eaten raw, but are more commonly sautéed with eggs or potatoes. Some people dislike the slimy texture of the pads, but extended cooking removes more water and sliminess.

The leaves and pads have been eaten to help adult-onset diabetes. Some of the research on this plant for curing diabetes, as well as lowering cholesterol levels, has been documented in *Prickly Pear Cactus Medicine* by Ran Knishinsky. You can even buy pills made from the dried cactus if you dislike eating it.

The ripened fruits, once cleaned of their many tiny glochids, can be peeled and eaten. These fruits have been shown to cure urinary infections.

MINT

Wild mint is found along streams throughout North America. I make a hot tea from these sweetly fragrant leaves. Besides being a breath freshener, mint tea is effective for stomachaches and even for cases of mild food poisoning.

BUSHCRAFT

ALOE

Sometime in late 1978, my mother shared with me an experience she'd had with the aloe vera plant. She was a registered nurse who worked at a Pasadena, California, retirement home. A patient had been treated by the resident doctor for a burning rash-like condition with Atarax, cortisone and tranquilizers, but the rash persisted for about three months. The patient said she hardly slept during that time and the rash "burned like fire." Finally, out of desperation, she allowed my mother to apply the gel of the fresh aloe vera juice to the rash, and she experienced an immediate cooling sensation. The rash was nearly gone eight hours later.

When the doctor arrived, my mother told the doctor that the patient's rash had cleared up, and she admitted to having applied aloe juice. The doctor examined the patient, and, without commenting on the aloe, told my mother, "It's good the medicine finally worked."

She documented over many years the use of aloe gel for such conditions as sunburn, skin sores, diaper rash, bedsores, even poison oak. Today, its uses are a broad mix of antibiotic, astringent, pain inhibitor, emollient, moisturizer, antipruritic (itching reducer), as well as a nutrient.

Aloe vera is useful for a wide range of skin problems.

ALOE IS WELL KNOWN TO ALLEVIATE PAIN FROM BURNS AND SORES.

BUSHCRAFT

Garlic is great for preventing infections, among other uses.

Garlic shoots take about nine months to mature.

GARLIC AND ONIONS

In a variety of tests, garlic and onion have been shown to reduce cholesterol, reduce high blood pressure, and reduce the incidence of flu.

Alan Tsai, PhD, a researcher with the Michigan School of Health, has tested rats and humans for the effects of garlic on cholesterol levels. He fed test groups high-cholesterol diets, with one group receiving garlic. Those who included garlic had cholesterol levels that rose about 4 percent, as opposed to those without garlic, whose cholesterol levels rose 23 percent. Dr. Tsai also noted that the incidence of cardiovascular and other diseases is lower in countries whose populations consume large amounts of garlic.

Though there are countless studies pertaining to the effects of garlic and onions on the human body, it may still be some time before doctors make conclusive statements, such as consumption of garlic will prevent high blood pressure. This is due to the complexity of high blood pressure, its various causes, and the fact that no two people are alike.

I eat garlic (and its many relatives, like chives, onions, shallots and leeks) just about every day. Though I buy garlic cloves from my local farmers market, the fresh leaves of wild onions and garlics can be picked just about anywhere throughout North America.

I have also used freshly crushed garlic cloves directly applied on wounds to prevent infection—another benefit from this group of plants.

—*Christopher Nyerges*

Christopher Nyerges has been leading ethnobotany classes for over 40 years. He is the author of *Guide to Wild Foods and Useful Plants*, *Foraging Wild Edible Plants of North America* and other books. He can be reached at schoolofself-reliance.com.

BUSHCRAFT

BENEFITS OF TRACKING

Tracking isn't just a way to put food on the table. It can save lives, too. Plus, it can be fun.

BE PREPARED JUST IN CASE SOMETHING HUNGRY IS ACTUALLY TRACKING YOU.

Learning to identify animal tracks will help you avoid potential threats.

BUSHCRAFT

WOULD YOU LIKE TO SEE MORE OF WHAT IS GOING ON AROUND YOU? WOULD YOU LIKE THE ABILITY TO READ THE EARTH LIKE A BOOK? THE TALENT TO TRACK IS NOT SOMETHING THAT SOMEONE IS BORN WITH, BUT RATHER A SKILL THAT TAKES HEAPING AMOUNTS OF DIRT TIME TO DO WELL. THE BEAUTY OF IT IS THAT TRACKING SKILLS CAN BE UTILIZED TO TRACK GAME YOU ARE HUNTING, APPREHEND A CRIMINAL IN A RURAL OR URBAN ENVIRONMENT, OR TO TRACK LOST PEOPLE FOR SEARCH-AND-RESCUE PURPOSES.

LOOKING FOR SIGNS, SEARCHING OUT TRACK TRAPS

We can increase the probability of finding more tracks by going to areas in which we are likely to find them. If I lose tracks, I will often go to one of these areas to look for them. These areas of high probability are often referred to as "track traps." Some of the more obvious ones are watering holes, feeding areas and common travel corridors. These areas also have soft ground to capture tracks. All animals, including humans, need water and food. By going to these areas, you increase the chance of finding more sign (evidence of passage).

CHANGE YOUR POINT OF VIEW—A LOT

The ability to see more tracks is multifaceted. It is important to understand how shadow and light are seen in tracks. To see more tracks, make sure you are looking for them as you walk—and change your elevation from time to time. Changing elevation will allow you to see better angles of the tracks themselves. You can practice this by standing near a known track to get more detail. By changing your perspective, you will see different parts of the track more clearly. Changing your elevation will also give you a different perspective, which will allow your eye to pick up a track that had not been seen yet. A very common tracker adage is Sun-Track-You. This simply means that whenever it is possible, place the track between you and the sun (light source) when attempting to examine it. This allows you to see more of the track because of the shadows cast in it.

OCCASIONALLY LIMIT YOUR VISION

It sounds counterintuitive, but this is a tactic I use regularly. While viewing an area in an attempt to locate sign, I cup my hands around my eyes to direct them from the sun and to focus my vision and attention on smaller areas. In this manner, I do not have to take in as much material. This allows my brain to catch up with what my eyes are transferring to it.

If tracking in a group, it's important to make sure nobody spoils the trail.

BUSHCRAFT

BEING ABLE TO TRACK COULD MEAN THE DIFFERENCE BETWEEN A FULL OR EMPTY BELLY.

Some animals have a direct register. That occurs when the back foot nearly replaces the front in the typical gait pattern.

TRACK: WHAT DO WE SEE?

OUTLINE
The perimeter and shape of the track or partial track.

COLOR
Different transferred items (leaf to field) will often be noticed due to color differences.

VALUE
Lightness or darkness of colors in the track.

SHAPE
The overall shape of track and the individual shapes of the parts of it as well.

TEXTURE
The area of the track (disturbance) will vary from the area around it (baseline).

RHYTHM
Multiple tracks of all animals have rhythms and gait patterns.

BUSHCRAFT

IT'S MORE THAN WHAT IS ON THE GROUND

There are many more pieces of sign than just a track in soft ground. Aerial sign is sign that you find above ankle level. This includes broken branches, displaced cobwebs and more. Intangible sign are things that may not be obvious, such as dogs barking, alarmed animals like deer, or a bee's nest that's stirred up.

AGING SIGN

In the common lore, this is one of the most frequently misrepresented aspects of tracking. Unless you have seen your quarry making the track and know when it occurred, it is virtually impossible to give a specific time of when a track was made. What you can do is understand the timing of it based upon other factors. An example would be you noticing that a deer you are tracking steps onto the tire tracks you made when you drove into the area. This means the deer came that way after you came in. Nature events, like rain, can also give a tracker the ability to gather a relative time frame of when a track was made.

USE SOME TOOLS

There are three tools that help me as a tracker. The sun does not always cooperate, so a quality tactical flashlight is a good device for a tracker to have. It can provide the light to see the detail in a track. A monocular also limits your vision. You can utilize the monocular to get more specifics in front of you. This gives you the benefit of seeing the finer points without contaminating the track line. I also suggest a GPS as a preemptive measure for practice.

—*Craig Caudill*

Craig Caudill is the owner/chief instructor of Nature Reliance School and author of *Extreme Wilderness Survival* and *Ultimate Wilderness Gear*. He has taught mantracking skills to federal, state and local law enforcement, search and rescue teams, and to the public. The Nature Reliance School instructor cadre are all avid trackers and incorporate aspects of it into all their survival, land navigation and mantracking courses throughout the year.

LEARN BY DOING

Books and videos are helpful, but the only way you'll learn to track is to get outside and practice. Find a track and follow it as far as you can. If you lose it, try again.

BUSHCRAFT

WHEN I WAS YOUNG, I SPENT MOST OF MY SPARE TIME IN THE FOREST, EITHER BY MYSELF OR HANGING OUT WITH THE NEIGHBOR KIDS. WHILE WE OFTEN PLAYED ARMY OR SOMETHING SIMILAR, OUR ACTIVITIES USUALLY REVOLVED AROUND BUILDING FORTS OF DIFFERENT SIZES, SHAPES AND STYLES. IT WAS NOT UNTIL I WAS A LITTLE OLDER THAT I REALIZED THAT MANY OF THOSE FORTS WERE ACTUALLY VERY SIMILAR TO EXPEDIENT WILDERNESS SHELTERS.

If you've got the right tools, you'll find it easier—and quicker—to build a shelter.

If you find yourself in a situation where you'll need to spend the night outdoors, it's important to get to work on your shelter sooner rather than later. It takes time to gather your materials and build everything. You'll want to get it done while you still have enough light to see what you're doing.

The focus here is on shelters that can be made with a minimum amount of gear or supplies. However, any time you head out on the trail, you should have certain items with you that will make your situation easier, should you unexpectedly have to hunker down for the evening.

KNIFE A sharp cutting tool will allow you to cut branches to size, make notches in them, and help create tinder with wood shavings. It might be your most valuable survival tool.

CORDAGE While it is certainly feasible to weave cordage from plant material and other sources, it is far more efficient and easier to have a hank of cordage or something similar with you.

EMERGENCY BLANKET Keep a good-quality emergency blanket in your pocket, just in case. If it gets cold, you can wrap it around you for warmth; if it's hot, it can be used for shade.

FIRE KIT Not every emergency night out will require fire. But even if the temperature is mild and you don't need to boil water, a small campfire can still be comforting.

Every emergency shelter has pros and cons. As with any aspect of survival planning, there is no one-size-fits-all solution. Let's take a closer look at two survival shelters.

LEAN-TO

The lean-to shelter is one of the simplest to make. Find two trees that are between 4 and 6 feet apart. Ideally, the trees will have branches a few feet off the ground. Locate a sturdy stick long enough to stretch between the two trees. It should be at least a couple of inches thick. Lash the branch in place between the trees about 4 feet off the ground.

After the crossbar is in place, lay leafy branches from the crossbar down to the ground at an angle on one side, and leave the other side open. Continue piling on branches and forest debris to make for a somewhat insulated roof. You can also lean branches on the shorter sides to create walls to further insulate the shelter.

The lean-to goes together quickly, provided you can find the proper size branches. When it is built properly, it can provide a decent roof over your head and protection from rain, wind and other elements. However, because it doesn't retain heat as well as some other shelters due to the open side, it isn't the best option for cold conditions.

If you build a fire, do so near the front of the lean-to and use a reflector wall behind the fire. This will help direct the heat toward your shelter.

SHELTER LOCATION

The location of your shelter is just as important, if not more so, than the structure itself.

✖ Avoid ravines and gullies, as that's where cold air will sink.

✖ Avoid sheltering under large branches that could possibly fall on you.

✖ Avoid areas that are likely to wash out when it rains.

✖ Avoid any areas that are damp.

✖ Avoid building your shelter on or near poison ivy or poison oak.

✖ Avoid ant nests, ground bees and other bugs.

✖ Avoid the tops of ridges and other areas open to high winds.

BUSHCRAFT

DEBRIS HUT

The debris hut traps your body heat to keep you warm. When made properly, it is not a roomy shelter.

Choose the location and lay down on the ground. Mark a perimeter around your body from head to foot, about 5 inches away from your body on all sides. You can either draw a line in the dirt or use small sticks and drive them into the ground like little stakes.

Next, gather your materials. You'll need a ridgepole that is about a foot longer than you are tall. It should be sturdy and fairly straight. Look for branches a few feet long that you can use for the frame. Finally, gather up some debris. That will consist of leaves, possibly with some pine needles and pine boughs mixed in.

Start by making a pile of debris about 6 inches thick inside the outline you made. This will insulate your body from the ground. Use forked sticks driven into the ground at the head and foot to suspend the ridgepole above the middle of your pile. It should be just high enough to allow you to roll over on your pile without hitting it. Keep in mind that the head end of the ridgepole is where you'll be crawling in and out. You'll want those forked sticks angled far enough apart that you can squeeze between them.

Place your framework along one side of the ridgepole. Angle them down to the ground, trying to get as close as you can to that perimeter line you established. When you have one side done, roll into the half-built shelter and see how it fits. Once you're happy with it, add the ribs to the other side.

As you build the framework, start piling on more debris. Doing so as you go along will help keep the ribs in place. Continue adding debris until the pile is at least a couple of feet thick. The more debris you add, the better insulated the shelter will be.

When you're ready to turn in for the night, wriggle your way into the shelter, feet first.

If you have a pack, you can leave it just outside the shelter, then pull it in and use it to plug the entrance. If you don't have a pack, leave a pile of debris within reach and use that. It won't be perfect, but it should suffice for the night.

It is recommended that you try building these shelters a few times before you truly need them to survive.

This debris hut appears larger than it is inside, due to all the dried leaves.

WITH A SNUG FIT AND LAYERS OF LEAVES, A DEBRIS HUT WILL KEEP YOU WARM AND DRY.

BUSHCRAFT

WOODSY WOMEN

Girls can get outside and play in the dirt, too.

AROUND SIX YEARS AGO, AFTER RETURNING FROM A SIX-MONTH STAY OFF-GRID IN NEWFOUNDLAND, CANADA, I STARTED LEARNING AND PRACTICING BUSHCRAFT AND BACKWOODS CAMPING SKILLS. I ASKED MY BROTHER, WHO HAS BEEN AN OUTDOORSMAN FOR DECADES, FOR TIPS. HE SAID, "YOU KNOW YOU'RE PRETTY GIRLIE, RIGHT?" I REPLIED, "YES, BUT YOU KNOW I'M ALSO PRETTY STRONG, RIGHT?"

SPENDING TIME IN THE WILDERNESS IS A GREAT WAY TO BURN CALORIES AND CENTER YOURSELF.

BUSHCRAFT

CLOTHING AND GEAR

Choosing appropriate clothing, footwear and gear can make your time in the woods more enjoyable and safer. Clothing is our first line of shelter. It protects us from the elements and the environment. Select appropriate attire carefully and dress according to the weather. In warmer weather, consider insect and sun protection. In cool weather, I dress in layers, starting with a synthetic, wicking base layer. To that, I add a woolen middle layer and then a waterproof, windproof outer layer. Add or remove layers as necessary throughout the day.

In warm weather, I carry a cotton shemagh, which is a large square scarf. In cool weather, I switch that out for a wool scarf or pashmina. I can wrap it around my hips to keep my bottom and lower back warmer. It's a nice, multifunctional addition to my kit, and can be used as a shawl, head cover, sling, bandage material or to carry items.

Choose function over fashion. Wear clothing that is comfortable and durable—it needs to be sturdy enough to withstand outdoor activities without

He suggested some reading materials, gear and a few online groups to help me get started. Some Canadian friends also gave me bushcraft "homework" to practice. I began researching, collecting my kit and practicing skills. I became active in the bushcraft community and started attending, then eventually hosting, gatherings. It's been an amazing adventure.

I realize everyone's journey is unique. But venturing into the woods, and into the online bushcraft community, is different for women. We face different issues and challenges. Fortunately, there are ways to address them.

ripping or tearing easily. I prefer natural materials, such as wool, in neutral colors. Synthetic materials tend to collect burrs and thistles and can melt if hit with a spark from a fire. Lots of adequately sized, well-placed pockets are a plus. Finding appropriate clothing that fits my larger female shape comfortably, without restricting movement or chafing, can be difficult. Often, I buy men's clothing, then make alterations so they fit. Hiking skirts can be a comfortable alternative and they make "answering nature's call" easier.

Most of my gear is unisex or from the men's department. Not all gear for women is as sturdy or high-quality as similar gear for men—for example, lady's work gloves tend not to be sturdy enough. I get men's gloves that fit my palm comfortably, then modify them for a bit more length in the fingers.

When general anatomical differences are significant, look into female-specific clothing or gear. Women are proportioned differently from men—we tend to have longer leg-to-body ratios, shorter torsos, shorter arm lengths, lower centers of gravity, smaller hands, narrower heels—and our cores, fingers and feet tend to get cold more easily.

> **WE MAY NEED TO MODIFY HOW WE DO THINGS TO COMPENSATE FOR SIZE OR STRENGTH. USE BODY MECHANICS TO YOUR ADVANTAGE.**

SHOES/BOOTS

Appropriate footwear can help reduce the risk of mechanical injuries and blisters. Whatever type you choose, makes sure it fits your foot well. In general, women's feet are wider through the ball of the foot, while being narrower in the heel. Our ankles tend to be more slender. Sometimes I've been able to use men's boots by adjusting my lacing pattern to keep the heel snug, without squeezing the front and instep of my foot. My feet tend to get cold, so I allow extra room for thick socks when choosing my winter boots. I also carry an extra set of thick wool socks to sleep in, or in case my other socks get wet.

BACKPACKS

Packs designed for women generally have a shorter torso, curved shoulder straps to fit better through the bust, smaller waist belts and extra padding for comfort and to reduce rubbing. I modified my chest strap to fit comfortably. Some women may be able to wear the waist belt on a unisex pack above their hip bones; this doesn't work for me—I'm extra curvy. I use a men's pack with a women's waist belt for a better fit. When loading my pack, I put heavier items at the bottom so the waist belt can support more weight through my hips. When trying on packs, put weight in them. Take the time to adjust the yoke, straps and

BUSHCRAFT

TAILOR YOUR PACK WEIGHT, CONTENTS AND STYLE TO YOUR NEEDS AND COMFORT LEVEL.

42 BACKWOODS SURVIVAL GUIDE

Views like this are worth the sweat it takes to get there.

BUSHCRAFT

belts. A good outfitter should be able to help you find a pack that fits your frame. Make sure it's comfortable when you move as you normally would in the woods.

SLEEPING BAGS AND PADS

A good night's sleep is invaluable. Sleeping at a comfortable temperature helps. Opt for a sleeping bag rated for a temperature at least 20 degrees colder than the one you expect to be sleeping in. If you are a ground sleeper, you may prefer a women's sleeping bag or pad, which usually has more insulation in the hip and foot areas, and may be roomier in the hips. I prefer a hammock-and-tarp setup. My winter underquilt (a quilt suspended under a hammock for bottom insulation, in place of a sleeping pad) has additional fill through the torso. A wool blanket added inside my hammock also helps keep me warm.

BALDRIC RIGS OR BELTS

Carrying a knife on my belt doesn't work well for me. The handle digs into my ribs and I can't see the sheath over my chest, which can be dangerous when returning my knife to its sheath. A baldric rig, which is a type of cross-body belt or shoulder strap, makes carrying my tools much easier, and the strap is adjustable to fit over a coat, if needed.

CREATING A PLACE FOR PRIVACY

While camping with others, I use my tarp or a rain poncho to provide privacy for toileting, taking care of hygiene needs or during clothing changes when the terrain doesn't naturally provide seclusion.

HOW TO ACCOMMODATE SHAPE, SIZE AND STRENGTH DIFFERENCES

Our smaller builds and relatively lower muscle mass means we may need to modify how we do things. Flexibility may help. For example, I have an easier time getting a bow drill ember by adjusting where I place my board, bow and spindle. Keeping the whole set to the outside of my right leg keeps my chest out of the way. I've also modified how I hand-drill, and find that longer spindles help. I use leverage to break tree limbs by wedging them between trees rather than chopping when possible. Use a saw rather than an ax if it's safer. Consider your strengths. Know your limits. Find what works for you.

HYGIENE

Anticipate your needs. Spray some antiperspirant or apply diaper rash cream on your lower chest or on other areas that may collect perspiration. This can prevent or minimize rashes or chafing when it's hot. You may want to add castile soap, antifungal cream and tampons to your kit.

SAFETY

Here in the Midwest, I'm more concerned about unfriendly two-legged critters than wild animals, especially when I'm out alone. Trip pre-planning is always important. Be observant, and know what's going on around you. Camp with friends if possible. If you're camping alone, consider carrying bear spray or a firearm. Perimeter alarms may be useful, especially if you'll be base-camping solo. And always make sure someone knows when and where you'll be camping.

An underquilt takes the place of a pad when you're using a hammock.

Choose an ax that's appropriately sized for you.

Try different knives to see what is most comfortable.

A baldric rig is similar to a belt, but can be worn across the body.

BUSHCRAFT

ONLINE GROUPS

The online community can be a good place to ask questions and learn from others who have experience. It's OK to just read the discussions if you aren't comfortable actively participating, especially when you are new. If a group isn't friendly and helpful, move on to another. Bushcraft groups are plentiful. Many are female- and beginner-friendly.

GATHERINGS

Gatherings are a lot of fun. They can be an excellent opportunity to learn new skills and get hands-on experience. I've met some wonderful people and learned a lot at gatherings. These are a fantastic way to benefit from the knowledge of more experienced people.

I know being a female in a historically male-dominated field can be uncomfortable for some women. Unfortunately, women aren't always welcomed or accepted around the campfire. I believe this has been changing. As more women have become involved in outdoor activities, more men have welcomed them.

Be aware, at gatherings you may see men letting their guard down and just relaxing with the other guys. If they are comfortable being themselves in your presence, they have probably accepted you into their tribe. Overall, I've found the community welcoming. Sitting around a campfire with a group of friends cooking chili, telling stories or busting out hand drill coals are some of my favorite things to do.

I love the simplicity, self-sufficiency and freedom this expertise has provided me. I've learned a lot already, but there are always new skills to acquire and old skills to refine. I'm grateful for my mentors and the others who have shared their experiences with me. It has been inspiring to see more women demonstrating great outdoors know-how and expertise on popular survival-based TV shows. They are helping to pave the road leading more women toward unpaved woodland trails. Getting back to nature is a wonderful adventure!

—*Tracy Apperson*

Tracy Apperson is the owner of Sparrow Rose Soap & Herbs and Indiana Bushcrafters. For more information, see her website—sparrowrosesoap.com— or visit Indiana Bushcrafters on Facebook.

Nothing beats the camaraderie of spending time in the wilderness with like-minded women.

BUSHCRAFT

IT'S WORTH IT!

As a woman in the woods, I'd like to share some of what I've learned to inspire more ladies to spend time out in nature; to help men understand issues women face while out in the woods; and to encourage outfitters to make better gear and clothing for females. Addressing these issues in advance will make things easier if you are new to wilderness living, or if you'd like to introduce the women in your life to wilderness adventuring in a way where they'll want to go back. Yes, it's dirty out there, and yes, there are bugs—but it's worth it for the beauty, tranquility and spectacular views. There's something about returning to nature that is healing.

Equip yourself well before you head out to explore the great outdoors!

49

BUSHCRAFT

MEET THE STAFF

This simple piece of wood has many uses.

A walking stick might be one of the easiest-to-acquire items for hiking. Just find a suitable branch and you're in business.

WOODEN WALKING STICKS ARE TRADITIONAL, AND ARE EASY AND FUN TO MAKE.

BUSHCRAFT

Many of us, picturing Gandalf on the silver screen, have picked up a thick branch, thumped the end on the ground next to us and proclaimed, "You shall not pass!" While playing this role might be chuckle-worthy at times, the venerable walking stick has many uses beyond pretending you are defending the realm against the Balrog in *The Lord of the Rings*.

Store-bought

Homemade

Store-bought folding

If you head to any decent sporting goods store, you'll find a wide array of walking sticks, most of them made of carbon fiber or aluminum. They typically come in pairs and are sometimes called trekking poles. While those can be useful, the walking aids we have in mind here are perhaps a little more traditional or old-school.

I've seen them made from a wide range of materials, from PVC to metal. My own preference is wood. It just seems to feel right and appropriate to use a wood walking staff when I'm on the trail. But choose whatever you'd like, whatever speaks to you. If you're going with wood, look for oak, hickory, ash or walnut. You want it to be strong but somewhat lightweight since you'll be carrying it with you for miles to come.

Every ounce we add to our load needs to be carefully considered. Nobody wants to carry more weight than absolutely necessary. What makes the walking stick worth the weight to your hiking load? Read on.

BALANCE AID

Perhaps first and foremost, a walking stick can help you negotiate uneven terrain. Sometimes a third leg, so to speak, can be very helpful, such as when walking over a hilly trail that is covered in loose dirt and gravel. Plant the end of the stick with each step to give yourself an added point of contact with the ground. And if you happen to twist an ankle or knee, having a staff will certainly be appreciated as you limp your way back to civilization.

CHECKING DEPTH

If you need to cross a creek or stream on your travels, it might be wise to use the stick to check for dips and hidden rocks. Of course, it will also tell you the depth of the water as you go along so you can decide whether it is safe to continue. There can be sudden depth changes that could prove rather troublesome and it would be nice to know about them before you step down. The stick can be used in a similar fashion when going through deep snow.

BUSHCRAFT

> MOST STORE-BOUGHT TREKKING POLES HAVE ADJUSTABLE HEIGHTS.

A pair of trekking poles works wonders for keeping your balance on questionable terrain.

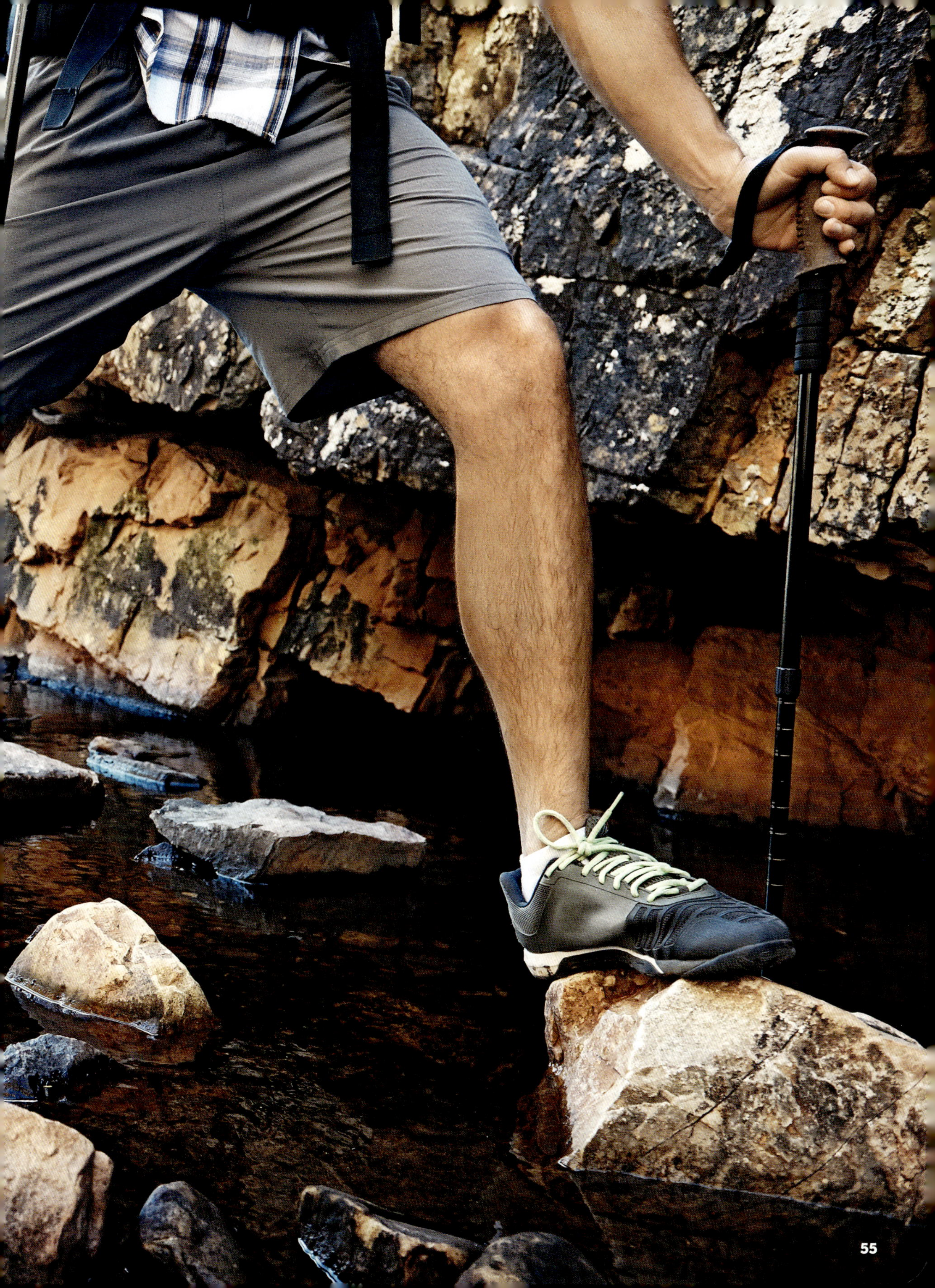

BUSHCRAFT

Walking sticks can come in handy as a pair of tent poles when you're hunkering down for the night.

56 BACKWOODS SURVIVAL GUIDE

REACHING TOOL

Should something fall in the stream, the stick can be used to reach and snag the item. Or, it can help you remove a pot from the fire by lifting it by the bail.

MEASURING

If you place markings on the walking stick ahead of time, you can use it as a reasonably accurate ruler. This could prove handy when fishing so you can ensure you're complying with size limits. It could also be useful when you're documenting the size or stride of animal tracks.

CAMERA STAND

While you won't be able to physically attach your camera or phone to your walking stick—not without some alterations and mechanical enhancements—it can still be used to steady your hand as you snap photos of the flora and fauna. Simply rest your camera or phone on the top of the stick and click away.

PATH CLEARING

The walking stick can be helpful when it comes to clearing the path in front of you. Use it to push branches out of your way, break through cobwebs or check for trip hazards in the underbrush.

SHELTER SUPPORT

If you end up having to spend an unexpected night outdoors, the stick can be used to assist in the construction of an expedient shelter. It could serve as the crossbeam in a lean-to, for example, or the main support in a debris hut.

BINDLE

Remember the vagabonds you used to see in old-time cartoons? The ones who walked with all of their worldly possessions in a wrapped-up handkerchief tied to a stick? That's not a bad way to carry a small amount of gear, should you be so inclined. It isn't nearly as good as a backpack, of course, but it'll work as an improvised carrying method.

DIGGING

Should you find it necessary to dig a hole, such as for a Dakota hole fire or even just a cat hole to go to the bathroom, having a stick at your fingertips can save your actual fingers.

BUSHCRAFT

Use a walking stick to check the depth of water or snow as you walk.

WALKING STICKS CAN KEEP YOU FROM STEPPING OVER AN UNDERWATER DROP-OFF.

BUSHCRAFT

USING YOUR STICK AS A DIGGING TOOL CAN PREVENT INJURED FINGERS.

SIZING THE STICK

While the size of the staff is largely a matter of personal preference, as a general guideline look for something that is tall enough to reach about to your sternum. That seems to be a good average for most folks. If it's too tall, it will feel cumbersome; if it's too short, you'll find yourself leaning over when you're using it to walk downhill. As for thickness, about an inch and a half works well for many people. If it is an inch or less, you may end up getting hand cramps from trying to grip it. Plus, you want the stick to be strong enough that you won't have to worry about it snapping. Thickness adds weight to the stick, however, so it is sort of a balancing act.

HUNTING AND FISHING

Don't plan on throwing a spear to secure dinner, not without an awful lot of practice. But you can still use the stick to obtain food. For starters, tie a line and hook to the end and use it as an improvised fishing pole. You could attach a spear point or just sharpen the end of the stick and use it to spear fish as well. Hint: Keep the point of the spear in the water to make it easier to hit the fish, rather than holding the spear above the water's surface. The spear point could also be used on land to procure meat by spearing small game or birds.

DEFENSE WEAPON

Provided it is simply a stick, without too much in the way of embellishments or additions, a walking stick is usually allowed just about anywhere, including in areas that are supposed to be weapons-free. With a little training in the use of a baton or staff as a weapon, it can be formidable. That said, leave the sword cane at home when you're headed to the airport, as TSA will definitely take it and you'll probably end up in a prone position on the floor. If you plan on regularly carrying your walking stick into businesses and such, it will likely go better for you if the stick is polished or looks finished in some way.

A walking stick is one of the simplest tools imaginable, yet one that has numerous uses. While you could just grab a new branch any time you head out on the trail, taking the time to customize one and making it truly your own is more fun.

—*Joshua Raines*

Joshua Raines has been tramping through forests practically since he was old enough to walk. He enjoys trying out new innovations with gear and technology, as well as getting back in touch with his roots and the traditions of those who came before.

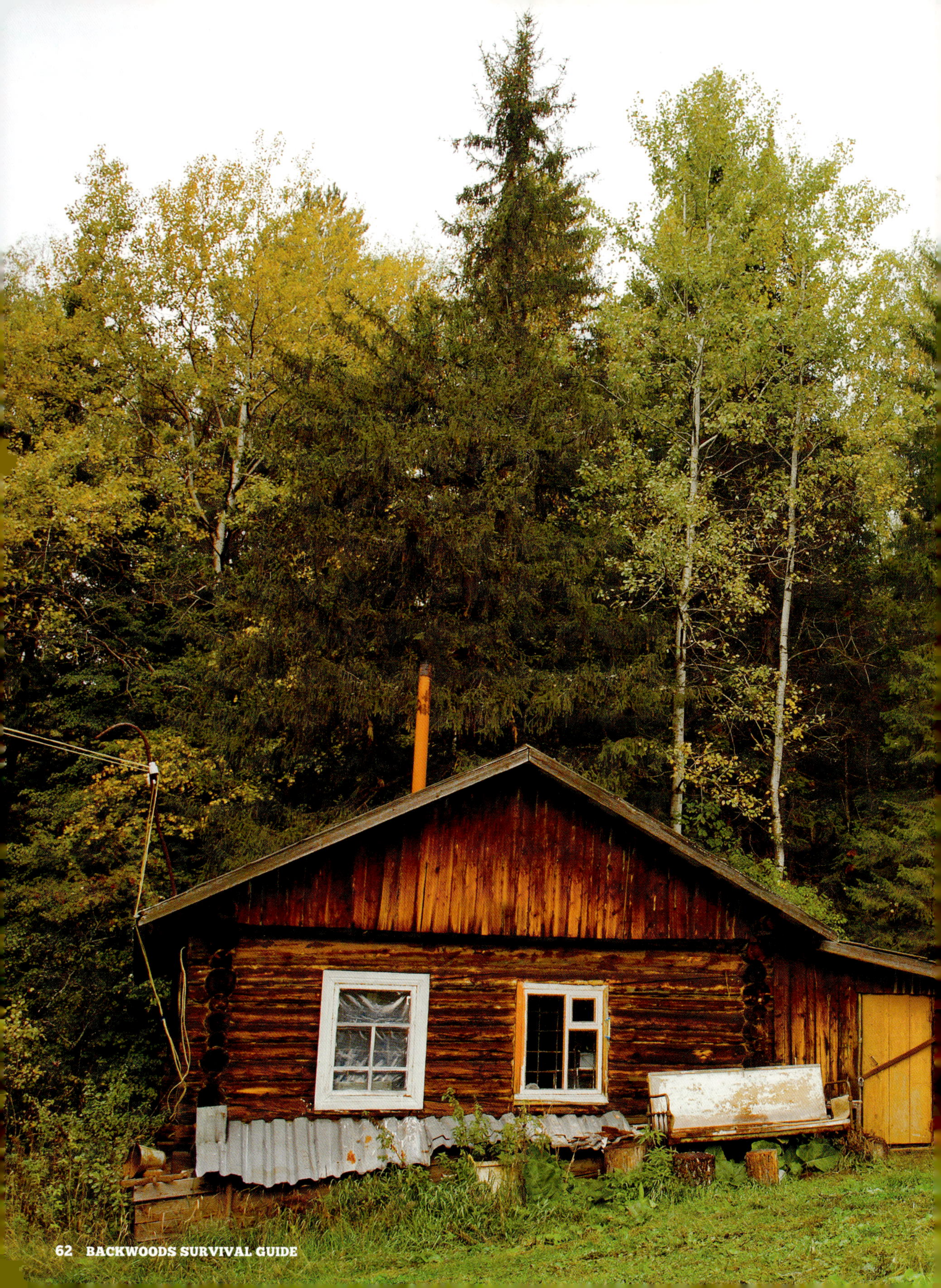

CHAPTER 2
HOMESTEADING

YOU DON'T NEED HUNDREDS OF ACRES OF LAND TO BE SELF-RELIANT.

HOMESTEADING

THE SURVIVAL GARDEN

Feeding your family from the backyard.

Plant in a sunny location—most vegetables need at least six hours of direct sunlight a day.

HOMESTEADING

GARDENING IS A FUN HOBBY AND CAN BE A GREAT WAY TO JUST GET OUTSIDE AND ENJOY SOME FRESH AIR. HOWEVER, PLANTING A TRUE SURVIVAL GARDEN REQUIRES A DIFFERENT APPROACH FROM YOUR USUAL BACKYARD PLOT.

The idea of a survival garden is to grow as much food as possible, making use of every inch of space. In addition, the plants should be ones that will produce crops at staggered times through the season, rather than everything in the garden ripening at once. You'll also want to have plants that give you the biggest bang for your buck, meaning ones that will give you a high amount of nutrients and calories.

As you go through the following suggestions, know in advance that not everything will grow everywhere. Climate, soil, length of growing season and even the location of the individual garden will dictate what grows well and what doesn't.

Also, concentrate your efforts on obtaining and using heirloom seeds. Many of the plants and seeds sold in the average big-box retail store are hybrids. While they will grow fine, the seeds saved from their produce might not grow at all. Or, if they do, they might be stunted or not produce vegetables or fruit. Heirloom plants are meant to grow true, generation after generation.

67

HOMESTEADING

THE USDA PLANT HARDINESS ZONE GUIDE CAN HELP YOU DETERMINE WHICH PLANTS ARE MOST LIKELY TO THRIVE IN YOUR AREA.

BEANS

Beans are high in protein, vitamins and calories, which makes them a great addition to the survival garden. They can be dried and kept on the shelf for years if they are stored properly. Plus, the plants add nitrogen back to the soil, which makes them a great selection for crop rotation. There are a ton of different types of beans, so select a few different ones that you know your family enjoys.

CARROTS

Carrots are packed with nutrition and they store very well for months if you keep them cool and out of the light. If you're in an area that doesn't experience harsh winter weather, you can even just leave them right in the ground. Cover them with a thick layer of mulch and simply dig up what you need when you need them. Because the green part of the plant above ground will die, make sure you mark the carrot locations for easy retrieval.

SUNFLOWERS

This one might seem like an odd choice at first. It certainly isn't a staple in the common garden. However, sunflower seeds make a tasty snack and are high in protein, which is something that can be lacking in a garden-centric menu. The seeds also have a great deal of vitamin E, magnesium and many other nutrients. As a bonus, they are somewhat high in fat—something that can become very important in a survival diet.

POTATOES

Potatoes get kind of a bad rap these days, as so many people are carb-conscious, but they should definitely be a part of the survival garden. They fill bellies and can be prepared in a large number of ways, from baked to fried and much more. Potatoes store very well for months at a time when kept cool and in the dark. You can grow several pounds of potatoes in a very small space, too, when you grow them vertically. Mound them or use a makeshift container so you can keep adding soil as the plant grows higher. When the season is over, dig up your bounty.

Do your homework to learn what crops will grow well in your climate.

HOMESTEADING

GARDEN SURPLUS CAN ALWAYS BE PRESERVED, BARTERED, DONATED OR SOLD.

Growing your own food is both rewarding and healthy.

HOMESTEADING

KALE

This so-called superfood is packed with important nutrients like vitamins A, C and K. Kale is a very hardy plant and can tolerate temperatures down to about 10°F. This makes it a wonderful addition to the survival garden, because you can keep greens in your diet for several months out of the year no matter where you live—and that can be essential when you can't just run to the store.

GARLIC

Garlic is a big part of any cook's repertoire. It adds flavor, of course, but it has many health benefits as well. It is a powerful weapon in fighting disease and infection, acting as a natural antibiotic. Many people also feel garlic is a cancer preventative, although the research is not conclusive.

PEPPERS

There are basically two types of peppers: sweet and hot. Bell peppers are in the sweet category. They are loaded with vitamin C and beta-carotene, both of which increase the longer you let the pepper sit on the vine, as it changes in color from green to yellow to red. Jalapeño and cayenne peppers fall into the hot category. While they have some health benefits, the hot peppers are typically more for adding flavor to the menu.

BROCCOLI

This is another healthy cool-weather crop. It should be started several weeks before the last frost. Depending on your climate, you might be able to get two rounds of broccoli by starting the second plants in early summer, planning for them to be ready in the fall. Broccoli is high in vitamin C as well as vitamin K.

BERRY BUSHES CAN BRING IN BIRDS AND OTHER CRITTERS, MANY OF WHICH MAY TURN OUT TO BE VIABLE DINNER OPTIONS.

BERRIES

There are several kinds of berries you can add for your survival garden. They are all healthy as well as delicious, from blackberries to strawberries. They can be eaten as is, or added to recipes for muffins and other baked goods. You can also dehydrate them for long-term storage. These plants also have a tendency to bring in birds and other animals, many of which might turn out to be dinner options.

TOMATOES

These are a great source of lycopene, which has been linked to reduced risks of heart disease and cancer. And for most people, the tomato is the No. 1 ingredient for homemade pasta sauces—and that's reason enough to make sure the survival garden is well-stocked with them. You can dry them for storage, and they can also be canned for later use.

CORN

Forget about growing sweet corn: It just doesn't store very well. Instead, look at field corn, also known as dent corn. You won't be using it for corn on the cob. Instead, you'll grind it into a flour and use it to make tortillas, bread and such.

Growing a garden is a great way to be more self-reliant—and the food can be incredible!

HOMESTEADING

PURCHASING SEED VAULTS

You've probably come across ads online for so-called seed vaults. These are large Mylar pouches filled with hundreds of heirloom seeds in dozens of varieties. The idea is that you can purchase this one package of seeds and you're all set for your survival garden. When the time comes, you tear open the pouch and plant everything you'll need.

The reality is, you have no way to know if the specific varieties included will grow in your climate. While some of them probably will, many might not. A far better plan is to research which varieties do best in your area, then buy the seed packets individually rather than as part of a larger collection.

HOMESTEADING

HARVESTING A PRECIOUS RESOURCE

Learn how to set up a basic rainwater catchment system and let Mother Nature reduce your water bill.

76 BACKWOODS SURVIVAL GUIDE

WATER IS EXTREMELY VALUABLE—AND IT LITERALLY FALLS FROM THE SKY.

Rainwater collection can be as simple or as complex as you wish. Just be sure to filter or disinfect the water properly.

HOMESTEADING

WHETHER WE ARE HOOKED UP TO A MUNICIPAL WATER SOURCE OR WE HAVE A WELL, OUR LIVES ARE TIED TO H2O. WE USE IT FOR SO MANY THINGS, FROM MAINTAINING OUR GARDENS TO CLEANING OUR BODIES. WATER IS TRULY ONE OF THE MOST VALUABLE RESOURCES IN THE WORLD, YET WE OFTEN TAKE IT FOR GRANTED. WHAT IF WE TURN THE TAP–BUT NOTHING COMES OUT?

An excellent way to get started with self-reliance is to set up a rainwater-harvesting system. Many people are surprised at just how much water can be collected in a single rainfall. For every square foot of roof, 1 inch of rainfall gives you 0.6 gallons of water. Let's say you have a 700-square-foot roof; here's the math.

700 x 0.6 = 420 gallons of water

No system is perfect and you won't be able to collect every drop, of course. But even if you manage only 75 percent, that's still over 300 gallons of water from just one rainfall.

There are three main components to any rainwater-harvesting system: catchment area; conveyance; and storage.

CATCHMENT AREA

The first step in the system is the catchment area. This is where the rain falls, which is typically the roof of the house or other structure. As we mentioned before, the size of the catchment area determines how much water you are able to collect.

As it falls, rain is usually very clean. However, once it

IF POSSIBLE, INSTALL GUTTERS ON ALL SHEDS AND OTHER OUTBUILDINGS.

IBC totes allow you to collect a couple hundred gallons of rainwater in one container.

HOMESTEADING

hits the catchment area, it will pick up contaminants. There are a few different types of roof materials that are in common use in the United States. In many parts of the country asphalt shingles are the most common. When rain hits these shingles, the water absorbs dissolved organic carbon (DOC). This isn't harmful to us, but when chlorine is added to the water, which is a common method of purification, the chlorine combines with the DOC to create chemicals that can cause cancer.

Metal roofs are a better option than asphalt, all other things being equal.

No matter what the roof material is, the rainwater will probably become contaminated with fecal coliform bacteria, which comes from the feces of warm-blooded animals.

CONVEYANCE

In almost all cases, a gutter system will be used to transport the water from the roof down to the storage containers. This system can be very simple or very complex, depending on your needs. At the most basic level, a gutter runs the length of the roof, collecting the water running down. A downspout

Keeping your gutters clean dramatically improves the efficiency of the whole system.

HOMESTEADING

on one end directs the water down to ground level.

Some systems will connect the downspouts on different sides of the structure, directing all of the water into one container. Others will have containers at each downspout. The downspouts should obviously terminate at the rainwater collection containers. There are devices you can install on the downspouts that will divide the water flow between two containers, should that be necessary for your system.

It is important to clean the gutters regularly. This will not only keep the system running more efficiently, it will reduce the contaminants in the water. If you're not able to get up there to clean the gutters yourself, either install some sort of gutter shield or pay the neighbor kid to climb the ladder.

STORAGE

Probably the most common container in a DIY rainwater-harvest system is a 55-gallon barrel, typically plastic rather than metal. Another one that can be found in some areas is a pallet tank or intermediate bulk container (IBC) tote. These hold 275 gallons and are typically used to transport bulk liquids or granulated substances.

Most garden shops and home-improvement stores sell ready-to-use rainwater-collection containers in a wide range of sizes and styles. Make sure whichever container you decide to use is food-grade, and was only ever used to transport food. If the container has been used, it will need to be thoroughly cleaned.

The container should be covered and fitted with screening of some sort where the water enters so as to prevent bugs, leaves and dirt from getting into it.

Many systems are set up with multiple containers connected in a chain; this will help capture as much rainwater as possible.

LEGALITIES OF HARVESTING RAINWATER

Sad to say...but there are some areas of the country that do not allow rainwater harvesting, though this is changing. Even if there are no laws on the books forbidding it, some homeowners associations (HOAs) don't allow it, possibly for aesthetic reasons if nothing else.

Do yourself a favor and make sure you won't be in violation of any laws, ordinances, or HOA rules before setting up a rainwater-harvesting system.

Of course, once the water is in the containers, you'll need a way to get it out to use it. Most folks install some sort of spigot at the bottom of the container. The container is placed on a raised platform, and gravity does the work.

WATER TREATMENT

Because the water will be contaminated by whatever is on the catchment area, it should not be consumed, used for critters, or used in the garden without first being treated in some way. It can, however, be used untreated to bathe, to wash the car, and for other cleaning purposes.

There are a variety of filtration options to consider. It is important to ensure that whatever method you choose will remove not only biological contaminants like bacteria but chemicals that may have leached into the water from the roof material. Not all filters will remove the same contaminants.

Note, though, that DIY purification methods like boiling will not remove any chemicals that may be present. In fact, boiling will increase the concentration of the chemicals, as some water is lost through steam.

A screen over the top of a rain-catchment bucket will reduce the amount of debris, like leaves, that falls in.

83

HOMESTEADING

Seed packets can have a wealth of information, such as ideal growing conditions and proper seed spacing.

PLANTING THE SEED OF SELF-RELIANCE

Being able to produce food is a big part of independence. It all starts with seeds.

SALAD & BULB

TRADING SEEDS CAN BE A FUN PART OF GARDENING. TRY SOMETHING NEW EACH SEASON.

HOMESTEADING

PROPERLY SAVING SEEDS SO THEY ARE AVAILABLE THE NEXT GROWING SEASON IS CRITICAL. NOT ONLY WILL THIS SAVE YOU MONEY IN THE LONG RUN, BUT BY NOT HAVING TO PURCHASE NEW SEEDS EACH YEAR, YOU WILL GAIN A GREATER DEGREE OF AUTONOMY, BECAUSE YOU'LL HAVE STORED WHAT YOU NEED TO GROW YOUR GARDENS IN THE FUTURE.

If you start by planting heirloom varieties of crops, you'll be able to plant the seeds from the fruits and vegetables you harvest and have them grow properly. Hybrid seeds don't always produce viable fruits or vegetables.

Long-term seed storage does take a little time and effort—but it is necessary so you will be in a position to be able to feed your family the following year. Remember, this isn't anything truly new or revolutionary. Rather, we're just going back to the way things used to be done.

The enemies of seed storage are the same as with storing just about anything: heat, sunlight and moisture. Avoid storing them where the temperatures fluctuate, such as an outbuilding or garage. The ideal storage temperature is 40°F, though that might not be feasible for everyone. Even a standard basement, which is typically cooler than the rest of the house, is better than keeping them at room temperature all year long.

If you store seeds in the refrigerator or freezer, let them come back up to room temperature while still in the sealed container before you open it. This prevents condensation from forming inside the container and possibly fouling the seed packets.

Whenever possible, obtain seeds from local growers rather than big-box stores. Local varieties will grow better.

HOMESTEADING

Labels on vials (top row): WINTER TRITICAL, BUCKW[HEAT], FIELD CORN, SWEET CORN, POPCORN

LABELING SEEDS IS VERY IMPORTANT. MANY SEEDS ARE VERY SIMILAR IN COLOR AND SIZE.

Labels on vials (bottom row): FLAX, BROWN MUSTARD, YELLOW MUSTARD, RAPESEED (POLISH), RAPESEED (ARGENTINE)

Organizing your seeds is a wise investment of time and effort. It is the only way you'll know for sure what you have.

88 BACKWOODS SURVIVAL GUIDE

SEED COLLECTION

The first step is to remove the seeds from the plant. Sometimes, as in the case of pumpkins, for example, the seeds are pretty easy to find. With others, such as carrots, the seed pod isn't attached to the fruit or vegetable and you'll need to know what it looks like and where to find it. Yet one more reason why it's important to get started with gardening before it comes time to rely on your harvest for survival!

If the seeds are dry, shake them into an envelope or other container. I cannot stress enough the importance of properly labeling all seed containers immediately. It is far too easy to get distracted and then forget which container has which seeds. Even just a strip of masking tape and a pen will be sufficient for the time being.

Wet seeds, such as those collected from pumpkins or squash, must be dried before storage. Put them into a bowl and fill the bowl with water. Any seeds that float are dead and can be tossed into compost. Swish your hand through the seeds in the water several times to clean them off, then carefully pour off the water and the bits of pulp. Lay the seeds out to dry for several days. Old plastic cutting boards or baking sheets work great for this purpose.

Once the seeds are dry, they can go into a properly labeled container.

HOMESTEADING

DRYING SEEDS FOR STORAGE

Yes, we just talked about cleaning and drying seeds. There's a difference between drying and *drying*. If you plan on keeping seeds for more than a year, they need to be properly dried. What we want to do is remove any moisture without heating the seeds. Hot temperatures could kill them.

One approach is to leave the seeds sitting out on baking sheets or something similar and let evaporation do the job. This will work but it can be a pain to have countless sheets of seeds taking up valuable counter space in the kitchen.

A great way to dry seeds is to use the cellphone approach. What's a commonly suggested remedy if you drop your cellphone in water? Stick it in a bag of rice for a couple of days. Rice absorbs moisture like that's its job and it's going for employee of the month. The same principle will work with drying seeds.

Stop in at a dollar store and pick up some nylons. Cut them into sections to make small pouches. Fill these pouches with seeds, being very careful to keep track of what seeds are in each pouch, then knot them closed. Keep the knots somewhat loose so you can untie them easily.

Fill a jar about halfway with rice, place a few pouches of seeds inside, then cover with rice and close the jar. The seeds should be sufficiently dried in a couple of weeks.

A vacuum sealer can be used to remove the air from the seed containers before storing them. Or you can put the seeds into plastic bags and squeeze as much air out of them as you can. Use a container that is relatively rodent- and insect-proof, such as a cooler, and keep it in a cool and dark location.

DRYING RICE

Because rice absorbs moisture so readily, it may already have a small amount of water inside—and thus it may not be quite the desiccant it could otherwise be. You can fix this by baking the rice for 35 to 45 minutes at 350°F. This isn't absolutely necessary but it does increase the rice's efficiency. Put the rice right from the oven into a jar and seal it tight. Let it cool before using it to dry seeds (or your cellphone).

Dried seeds, beans and the like can be stored for long periods of time if well-dried and packaged correctly.

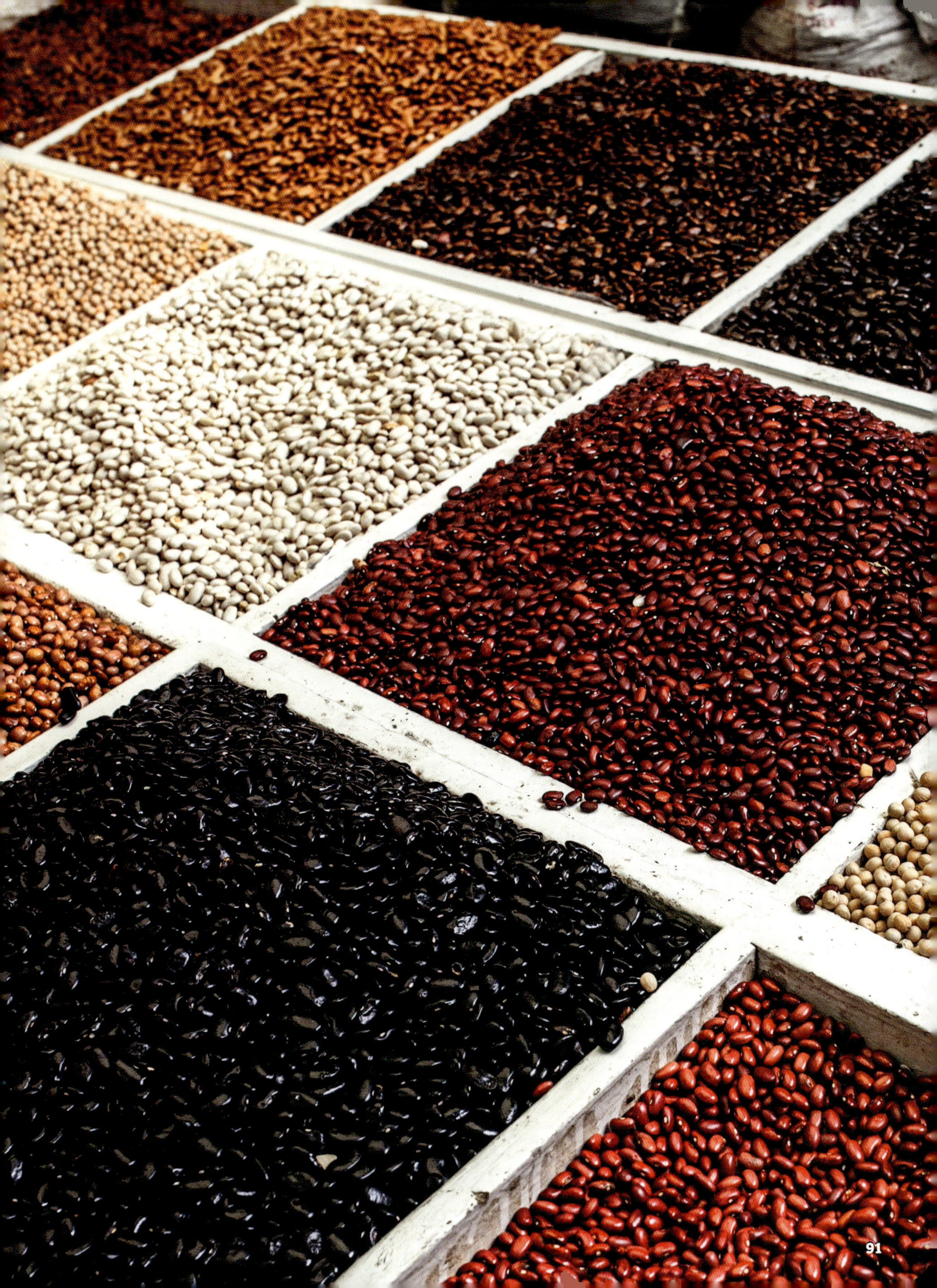

HOMESTEADING

An electric food dehydrator is a great investment. Fill it up, turn it on, and let it work while you do other things.

92 BACKWOODS SURVIVAL GUIDE

PRESERVING THE HARVEST

Preparing food for a long shelf life is a tradition that harkens back to the days when the pantry kept you fed through the winter.

HAVING AN AWESOME GARDEN IS ONLY HALF THE BATTLE. THAT PRODUCE ISN'T GOING TO LAST FOREVER WITHOUT SOME HELP FROM YOU. LEARNING HOW TO PRESERVE YOUR BOUNTY IS AN IMPORTANT PART OF SELF-RELIANCE. THESE SKILLS ALSO ALLOW YOU TO TAKE ADVANTAGE OF GREAT SALES AT THE SUPERMARKET OR FARM STAND. THERE ARE NUMEROUS METHODS YOU CAN USE—BUT NOT ALL FOODS ARE WELL-SUITED FOR EACH OF THEM. SOME OPTIONS REQUIRE SPECIAL EQUIPMENT, WHILE OTHERS ARE ABOUT AS LOW-COST AS YOU CAN GET.

HOMESTEADING

A root cellar should be below or partially below ground, like this one.

DEHYDRATING

Mold, bacteria and the other stuff that can cause food to go bad all require water to survive. Remove the water from the food and you can largely eliminate the problems. Dehydrating food can be done in a store-bought machine, in an oven, even outside. In fact, one way that works rather well in the summer months is to put the food on baking sheets in the back window of a car parked in the sun. Roll up the windows and let the sun do the work.

The goal of dehydration is to remove as much moisture as possible without cooking the food. It involves three basic elements.

1 Heat
About 140°F works well to remove moisture without cooking.

2 Dry Air
This absorbs the moisture from the food.

3 Air Movement
The dry air needs to be moved away as it absorbs moisture.

Start with ripe fruits and vegetables. Remove all seeds, pits, stems, and bruised or damaged areas. Cut it into pieces and rinse it all under cold water.

Most vegetables should be blanched before dehydrating. To blanch food, place it into boiling water for a few minutes, then put it into cold water to halt any cooking that is happening. Blanching stops any enzymatic reactions that might be occurring within the foods.

Fruits can be dipped into ascorbic acid rather than blanched. Mix one teaspoon of ascorbic acid crystals into one cup of water; dip the fruit pieces into it to prevent them from browning. Fruit juices high in vitamin C—such as lemon, orange or pineapple—can be used in place of the ascorbic acid mixture.

Place the pieces in a single layer on a baking sheet and put it in the oven at 140°F for several hours until done. Leave the oven door open a few inches to allow the air to circulate.

A food dehydrator can work faster and more efficiently, so it might be worth the investment for you. Follow the unit's directions for proper operation.

FREEZE-DRYING

This is, in some ways, like dehydration on steroids. Freeze-drying involves first freezing the food down to about -40°F. Moisture within the food will be frozen into ice crystals. The food is placed into a vacuum and warmed a bit. As it does, the ice evaporates. This results in a very shelf-stable food that lasts quite some time.

The other advantage to freeze-dried food is it loses very little of its taste and texture when it is reconstituted. It is light and easy to carry, too.

The downside is a home freeze-dryer is a pretty expensive proposition. Even a small model can run upwards of $2,000. But it can be a great option for large families or small groups to share.

ROOT CELLARS

Many vegetables will store just fine in a root cellar or something similar. There are numerous references online with instructions on how to build a root cellar, either in your basement or outside in the ground. Basically, they require adequate ventilation, humidity and darkness. A dirt floor will usually suffice for the humidity component. If, however, you find your veggies are shriveling up, you need to add more moisture to the equation. Misting them with a water bottle on a regular basis can help.

HOMESTEADING

NOT ALL PRESERVATION METHODS ARE PERFECT FOR ALL FOODS. LEARN TO USE A VARIETY OF TECHNIQUES TO BROADEN YOUR OPTIONS.

Light can lead to sprouting, so you want to eliminate it as best you can. Covering bins and boxes with cloth can help reduce light exposure while still allowing air circulation.

Ventilation is important, because many fruits and vegetables give off ethylene gas, which can cause produce to ripen or even spoil faster. Air circulation can help in that regard.

CANNING

There are two types of canning. Water-bath canning is suitable for foods that are high in acid, such as fruits and jellies. Pressure canning is used for low-acid foods, including meats, soups and vegetables.

Both types of canning utilize jars, rings and lids, all of which will need to be thoroughly cleaned and sterilized. Everything but the lids can be reused over and over, provided you take care of them. Some manufacturers make lids that can be cleaned and used again, but reports vary as to their reliability.

The great thing about home canning is the jars of food last a year or two, provided they are stored in a cool, dark place. Plus, they don't require anything special when it comes time to use the food. You don't need to rehydrate anything; just heat and eat. Of course, the jars aren't suitable for easy transportation, so you won't be packing any of them into an evacuation kit.

It is vitally important to follow all canning recipe instructions to the letter. A mistake in the processing could lead to botulism, which is a whole lot of no fun. An excellent resource is *The Prepper's Canning Guide* by Daisy Luther (2017, Ulysses Press).

Don't put all of your eggs in one basket and rely strictly on only one method of food preservation. Experiment with different techniques for different types of food and learn what works best for you and your family. Being able to save your own food for long periods of time reduces your reliance upon store-bought special survival foods.

Provided you are using good-quality equipment and you follow instructions precisely, canning food is a low-risk proposition.

HOMESTEADING

There is nothing like looking into your pantry and seeing shelves lined with colorful jars filled with food.

98 BACKWOODS SURVIVAL GUIDE

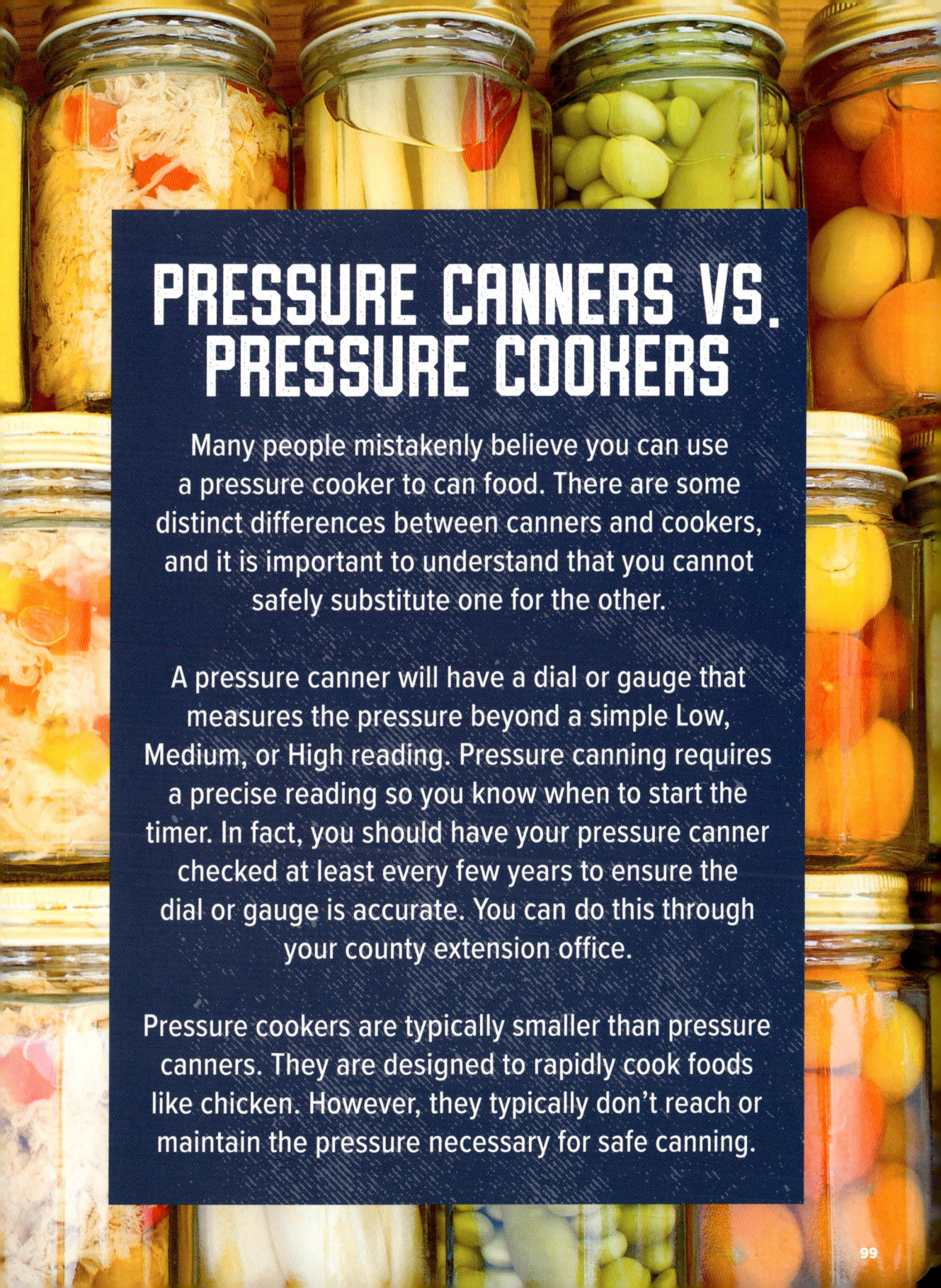

PRESSURE CANNERS VS. PRESSURE COOKERS

Many people mistakenly believe you can use a pressure cooker to can food. There are some distinct differences between canners and cookers, and it is important to understand that you cannot safely substitute one for the other.

A pressure canner will have a dial or gauge that measures the pressure beyond a simple Low, Medium, or High reading. Pressure canning requires a precise reading so you know when to start the timer. In fact, you should have your pressure canner checked at least every few years to ensure the dial or gauge is accurate. You can do this through your county extension office.

Pressure cookers are typically smaller than pressure canners. They are designed to rapidly cook foods like chicken. However, they typically don't reach or maintain the pressure necessary for safe canning.

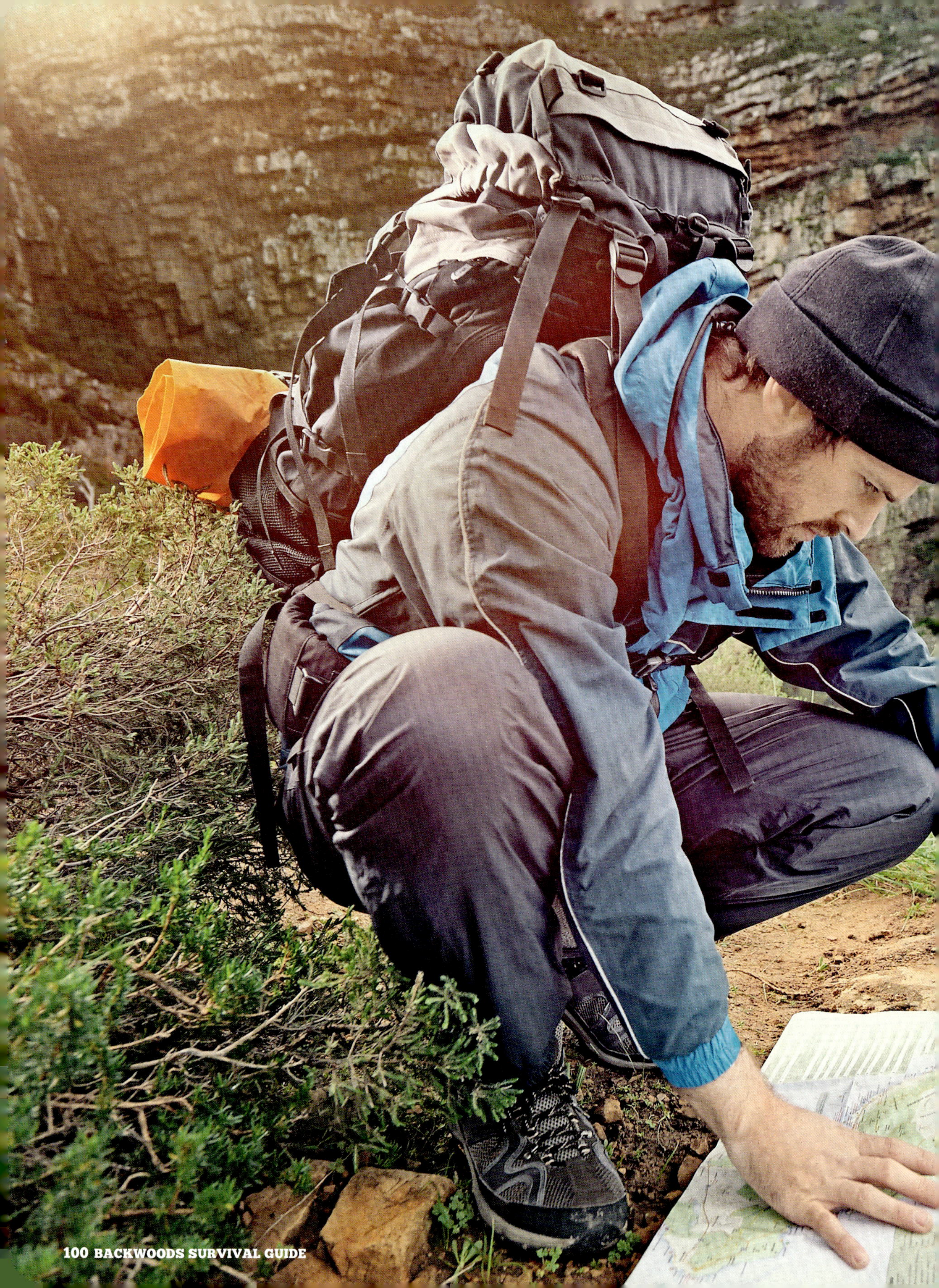

CHAPTER 3
SURVIVAL PLANNING

KNOWING WHAT YOU'LL NEED AND WHAT TO DO IN ADVANCE MAKES EVERYTHING EASIER.

PLANNING

HITTING THE TRAIL

Make sure you get back home safe.

Heading off to the outdoors is a great way to reduce stress and get some fresh air. Just take a few precautions first.

PLANNING

EVERY YEAR, HIKERS AND CAMPERS GO MISSING. SOME OF THEM EVENTUALLY RETURN HOME WITH A STORY TO TELL, WHILE OTHERS AREN'T SO LUCKY. MORE OFTEN THAN NOT, THEIR MISADVENTURES COULD HAVE BEEN PREVENTED OR AT LEAST MITIGATED THROUGH JUST A LITTLE PREPARATION AHEAD OF TIME.

The thing is, we get complacent. We may have gone out hiking a hundred times and the worst thing that happened was a little sunburn. But all it takes is one time when we should have zigged instead of zagged and things can go awry. It is far better to be prepared for the worst and have it never happen than to be caught with your proverbial pants around your ankles.

RESEARCH

Whenever possible, do your homework in advance. Check weather forecasts so you know what to expect with temperature and precipitation. Of course, the weather can change quickly, but even if it does, it will still likely be within an expected range for the location and time of year. It isn't probable that you'll experience a sudden blizzard in the middle of June while hiking in Florida, right? If you do, you will likely be facing bigger issues than the weather.

Know where you're going, which includes not just the driving directions to the site but the park or nature area itself. Download and print out trail maps and keep them with you once you reach the area. If official trail maps aren't available or perhaps don't exist, you can still print online maps from Google or another site.

Of course, a map is of very limited use without a compass. Learn how to use these tools together and make sure you have a compass with you when you hit the trail.

If you're heading to a county or state park or other official land of some sort, contact the appropriate agency to inquire as to the conditions there. Recent storms, for example, might have washed out some trails.

PLANNING

NEVER VENTURE INTO THE FIELD WITHOUT TELLING SOMEONE FIRST; LET THEM KNOW WHERE YOU'RE GOING AND WHEN YOU'LL BE BACK.

COMMUNICATION

Never venture out into the field without making sure at least one person knows about your travel plans. This doesn't need to be overly complicated. Simply tell a friend or family member where you are going, when you are leaving and when you plan to return. Set a date and time by which you will have checked in with them. If you miss that deadline, they should notify the authorities.

It's important that the person you are entrusting with this responsibility be someone you know will follow through—promptly—on their end. Too many people will hem and haw for hours about making the call to the sheriff's office, worried that they are jumping the gun and making a mistake. Meanwhile, you might be sitting in a debris hut, nursing a badly twisted knee or ankle and counting on your friend to make that call right away.

Of course, it is just as important that you follow through on *your* end. Check in according to your agreement, and also call them when you return to civilization so they don't end up needlessly sending out search parties.

The next element of communication is to leave information in your vehicle that the authorities can use to track you down if need be. Write up a complete itinerary, including the date and time you parked your vehicle, where you're headed, your planned route and the date and approximate time you plan to return to your vehicle. Naturally you aren't going to leave this information just displayed on your dashboard for any passerby to see, but you can place it in an envelope and leave it on your seat.

Leave your footprint on aluminum foil in that envelope too. This will hopefully help searchers track you down.

Leave info in your vehicle. This will help folks find you.

Keep an eye on the sky as well as the weather forecast so you're not caught by surprise by a storm.

PLANNING

> HIKING WITH FRIENDS CAN BE A FUN—AS WELL AS SAFER—BONDING EXPERIENCE.

Having one or more people with you means extra eyes looking out for risks and threats.

108 BACKWOODS SURVIVAL GUIDE

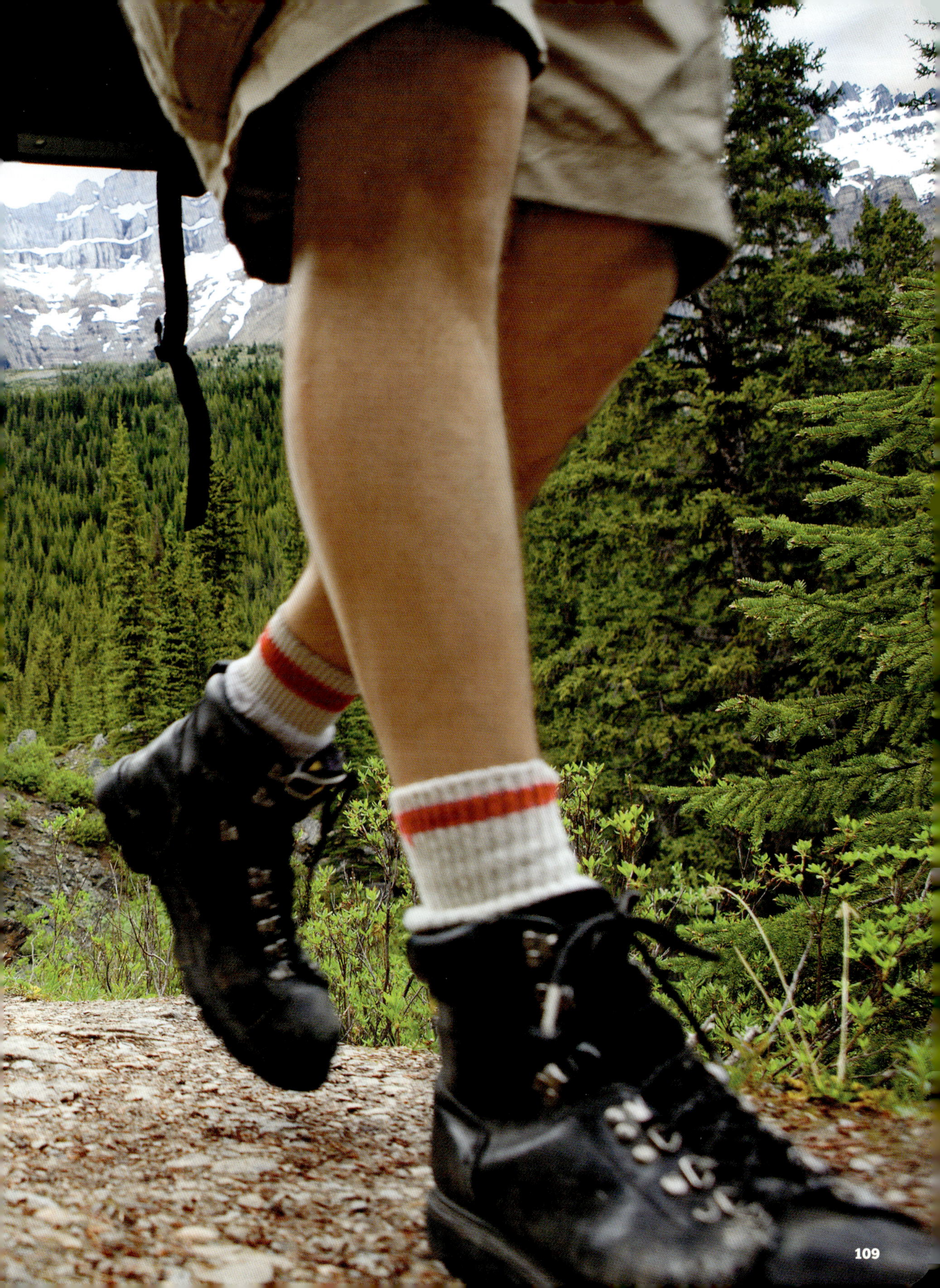

PLANNING

The basics don't weigh much or take up much space, but they might very well save your life.

110 BACKWOODS SURVIVAL GUIDE

CARRY A FEW ESSENTIALS WITH YOU EVERY TIME YOU HIT THE TRAIL, JUST IN CASE.

BASIC GEAR

It should be common sense to always carry some amount of survival equipment with you—but this is one area where many people fail. Sometimes it is because of ego and they are confident—perhaps overconfident—in their skills and they cannot fathom the possibility that they'll run into a situation they can't handle. Other times, it is just ignorance.

Even a simple day hike can take a turn for the worse. However, there are a few items that can be easily carried and will be of tremendous benefit should you end up having to spend a night outdoors unexpectedly.

First, a cellphone with a backup charger could be all you need to get help. While reception might be spotty in many areas, you could get lucky and find a signal. It certainly can't hurt to keep it with you, just in case.

A loud whistle should be a necessity for each person in your group. Wear it on a breakaway lanyard around your neck. This is one instance where plastic is preferred over metal. If you're hiking in cold weather, placing your lips on the metal whistle could turn out to be reminiscent of the frozen-flagpole scene in *A Christmas Story*. If you end

PLANNING

Once you've put your emergency supplies together, you'll be ready for your next trip.

up losing your way, a whistle won't tax your throat and the sound carries much farther than shouting. Three quick blasts is the universal signal for help.

An emergency blanket, sometimes called a space blanket, can help ward off the chill. Opt for a good quality one rather than something you'd find at the dollar store. After all, your life should be worth more than a buck. While the package will easily fit into a pocket, bear in mind that once you've opened it, you'll probably never be able to fold it back up that compactly again.

Despite commonly accepted wisdom, a fire isn't always a necessity for survival. If the temperature is mild, say in the low 70s, and you don't need to boil water to disinfect it, fire probably isn't a priority. That said, we don't prepare for days when the weather and overall conditions are fair and pleasant. We prepare for times when the weather is foul and we're in a bad spot. With that in mind, keep a disposable lighter or a ferrocerium rod in your pocket along with some ready-to-light tinder.

Just about every survival instructor will tell you to carry a knife with you at all times when you're in the field. A sharp blade is one of mankind's earliest tools. Choose the highest quality one you can find that fits your budget. A fixed blade sheath knife is stronger than, and thus preferable to, a folding knife.

It is certainly possible to weave plant fibers together and use them to lash together a shelter, but it is infinitely easier to just carry a hank of paracord or a similar rope in your pocket.

Finally, carry a small but good-quality water filter. Drinking untreated water can make a bad situation far worse.

All these items can easily fit into your pockets or in a day pack. Add them together and you're talking ounces, not pounds.

There are hundreds of hikers who have likely wished they'd done exactly these things before they headed out the door, not knowing it was the last time they'd see their loved ones again.

112 BACKWOODS SURVIVAL GUIDE

S.T.O.P.

Should the worst come to pass and you find yourself in the middle of nowhere without a clue as to how to get back to the trail or your campsite, don't panic. You'll be OK, as long as you keep your wits about you. The acronym S.T.O.P. is a mnemonic device that will help you remember what to do if you get lost.

S
STOP
The moment you realize you're not where you want or need to be, stop moving. Sit down and take some deep breaths to calm yourself down. Getting yourself all worked up and anxious isn't going to help anyone.

T
THINK
Try to mentally backtrack to where you went wrong. Keep in mind that the trail can look vastly different when you're coming from the opposite direction. Give thought to your options.

O
OBSERVE
Can you see any landmarks that can help you get back on course? Also note the environment, weather and time of day. If it's late afternoon, it might be best to hunker down for the evening rather than risk getting injured in the dark.

P
PLAN
Once you've calmed down, make a plan based on the information available to you. Adapt it as necessary to account for new information as you go along.

PLANNING

BACKCOUNTRY FIRST-AID ESSENTIALS

When you hit the trail, you are your own first responder.

A twisted or sprained ankle is a common injury in the field.

ANYONE WHO SPENDS TIME IN A REMOTE ENVIRONMENT NEEDS TO REMEMBER: NEVER ASSUME THAT HELP IS ALWAYS AVAILABLE. WE SHOULD PREPARE AHEAD OF TIME FOR POTENTIAL MEDICAL EMERGENCIES. OFTEN, WE MAY NEED TO PROVIDE RELIEF FOR MILD DISCOMFORT, SO AS TO NOT RUIN AN OUTING. HOWEVER, THE RISK OF SEVERE THREATS TO LIFE AND LIMB ARE EVER PRESENT IN THE BACKCOUNTRY. IN SOME INSTANCES, SWIFT ACTION AND THE RIGHT EQUIPMENT CAN MEAN THE DIFFERENCE BETWEEN LIFE AND DEATH. FOR SUCH SITUATIONS, KNOWLEDGE IS THE BEST MEDICINE.

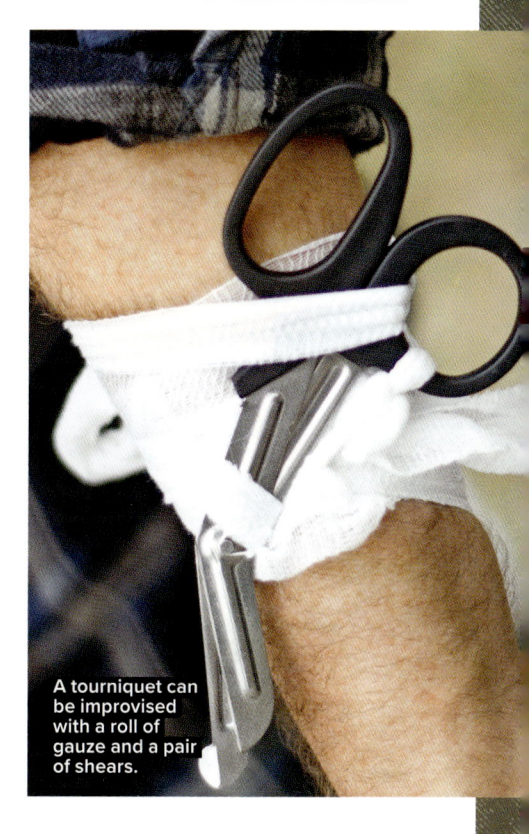

A tourniquet can be improvised with a roll of gauze and a pair of shears.

There are some situations that require advanced medical care. For these, it's best to plan your evacuation and seek definitive care as long as it is an option. Learn in advance what can and cannot be done in the backcountry.

For other medical emergencies that take place far from civilization, your first-aid kit must provide everything you need. (See our suggested kit contents on page 124.) Here are some of the most common backcountry emergencies you are likely to encounter:

PLANNING

BLEEDING

To control bleeding, first elevate and apply pressure. Using gauze is recommended, but even just holding your gloved hand over a deep puncture wound is beneficial. If the gauze becomes saturated with blood, add another piece on top; don't remove the already saturated dressing. For more severe bleeds, use a self-adhering bandage roll, like Coban or Vet Wrap, over the gauze to get a tight wrap around the injury. This technique is known as a pressure dressing. If the injury is so severe that a pressure dressing doesn't work, a tourniquet is needed. (Remember that tourniquets are for life-threatening bleeding only. Try direct pressure, elevation and a pressure dressing first.) While a commercial tourniquet is best, you can use a roll of gauze and trauma shears (see photo, page 115) or even a sturdy kindling-sized stick. Rotate the trauma shears as a windlass for tightening the tourniquet, and tie it securely with a second roll. If you do use a tourniquet, use a marker to note the time of application and prepare to get additional help.

SPLINTING

Unlike the world of modern medicine, backwoods survival is all about using what you have available. When dealing with strains, sprains and fractures, this can mean using sticks to stabilize an arm injury in the wilderness, or even splinting an injured leg to the uninjured leg in the event someone needs to be carried out on a makeshift stretcher. For the size and price, however, a single SAM splint will provide you many splinting options; it can even serve as a makeshift cervical collar in the event of a spinal or neck injury. Tongue depressors and a roll of cloth tape provide excellent splinting for finger injuries.

The goal of splinting is to immobilize the injured area, from the joint above to the joint below; or, if a joint is injured, from the bone above to the bone below. For instance, if you injure a forearm, immobilize it from the elbow to the wrist.

In addition to immobilizing the injury as best as possible, treat sprains and fractures with the R.I.C.E. formula (Rest, Ice, Compression, Elevation) and treat pain and inflammation with Tylenol (acetaminophen) and Motrin (ibuprofen). An elastic (Ace) bandage can be used to provide compression or to secure a splint, and an instant cold pack will further reduce pain and swelling. A triangular bandage can be used to secure splints or immobilize an arm or shoulder injury. Even cinching down on a boot lace immediately after rolling an ankle can mean the difference between being able to hike out on your own or not.

BURNS

Surprisingly enough, burns are easy to treat. Step one, stop the burning process. This may seem obvious, but reduce the skin temperature with cool water. Then, simply cover the burn with a dry sterile dressing and give it time. Vaseline gauze (sold in packaged strips) or a light layer of triple-antibiotic ointment can be beneficial for minor burns. Watch for signs of infection, and use anti-inflammatories to treat pain.

For large and severe burns, you must prevent fluid and temperature loss until evacuation. Use an emergency blanket to maintain core temperature. Rehydrate with an electrolyte drink if the person can drink.

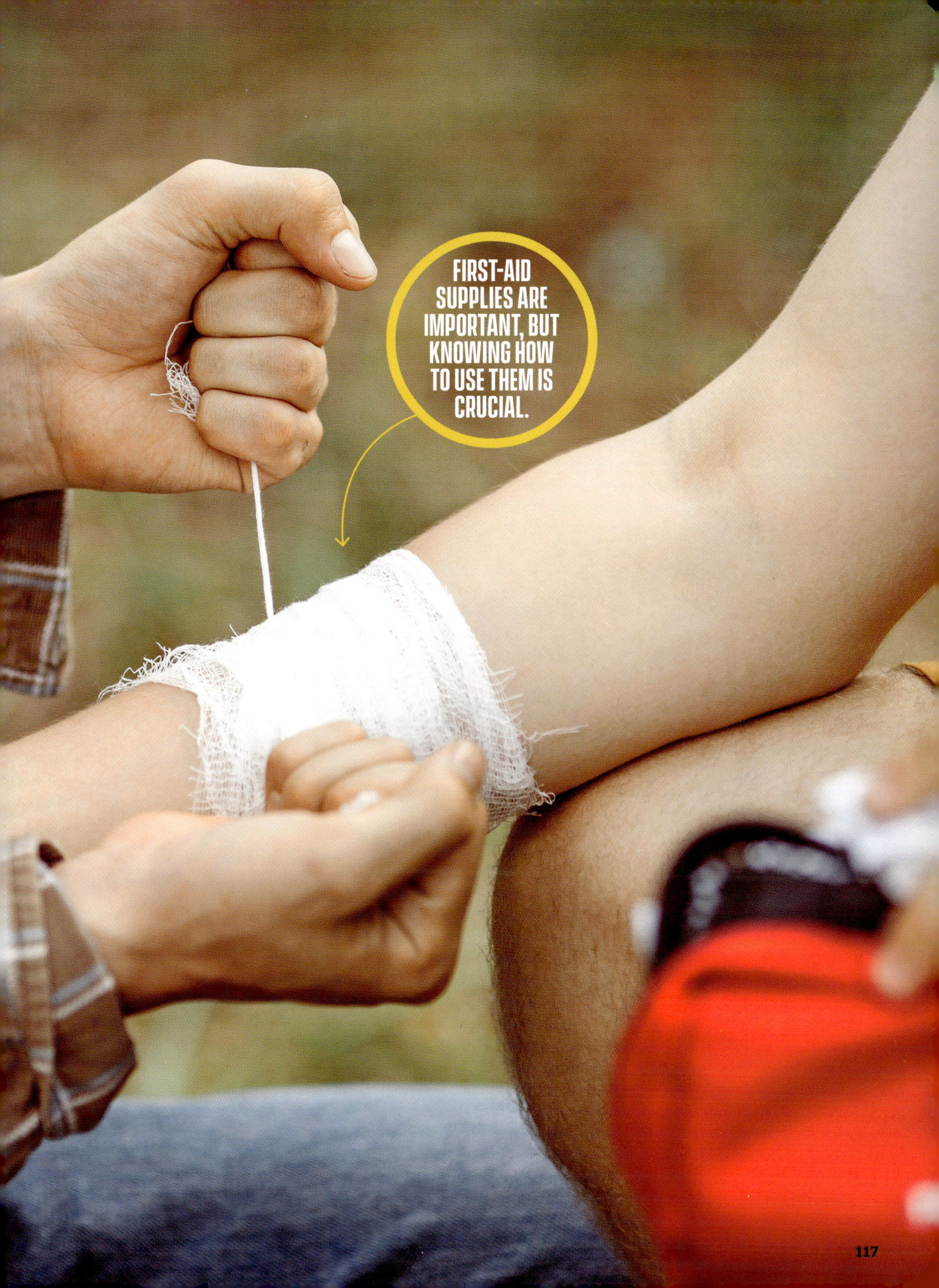
FIRST-AID SUPPLIES ARE IMPORTANT, BUT KNOWING HOW TO USE THEM IS CRUCIAL.

PLANNING

OLD SNAKEBITE REMEDIES, LIKE SUCTION AND INCISIONS, HAVE ALL BEEN SHOWN TO BE INEFFECTIVE. DON'T WASTE TIME; GET OUT AND GET THE ANTIVENIN.

BITES AND STINGS

For insect bites and stings, use Benadryl (diphenhydramine) orally to treat. The liquid gel-cap version can be broken open and used on the skin to provide topical relief as well. (Diphenhydramine also doubles as anti-nausea medication, and can be used to relieve cold or allergy symptoms, too.)

For the bite itself, including an animal bite, treat it as any other open wound—stop the bleeding, clean and irrigate with saline solution, disinfect with your antiseptic wipes, and cover with a clean dressing. One of the best things to do for any sting or bite is to draw a circle around the site with your marker (see photo, right). Do this every time you check the site to see the progression of swelling. It is helpful to positively identify the animal that bit you—but not at the risk of a second bite. If you believe you've been struck by a venomous snake, start planning your evacuation; time is of the essence. Splint the bitten area to immobilize it, and remove all jewelry and constrictive clothing. Remedies like suction, snakebite kits and incisions are not effective solutions: The most important thing is to get to a health-care center that can administer antivenin.

INTERNAL ISSUES

Sometimes, the things that injure us can't be seen. In the backcountry, these come predominantly in the form of parasites such as cryptosporidium or giardia that contaminate your water and cause gastrointestinal issues—stomachache, vomiting and diarrhea. Prevention is the best medicine—always boil your water, or use a combination of filtration and disinfection to treat your water before drinking or cooking—or even brushing your teeth. If you do come down with a case of vomiting and diarrhea, be aware of fluid loss. Losing too much for too long can cause hypovolemic shock, a serious medical emergency. The best way to keep this from happening is with medication and oral fluid replacement. For medications, use the Benadryl in your kit to prevent vomiting at the earliest sign of nausea; once you are consistently vomiting, it is unlikely for the medication to digest and become effective. For diarrhea, Imodium (loperamide) works best. For heartburn, use Zantac (ranitidine); it doubles as a mild antihistamine for allergic reactions, if you run out of Benadryl. Keep several salt and sugar packets in your kit to make an electrolyte-replacement drink. Mix 1 liter of disinfected water with 6 packets (6 teaspoons) of sugar and 4 packets (½ teaspoon) of salt.

118 BACKWOODS SURVIVAL GUIDE

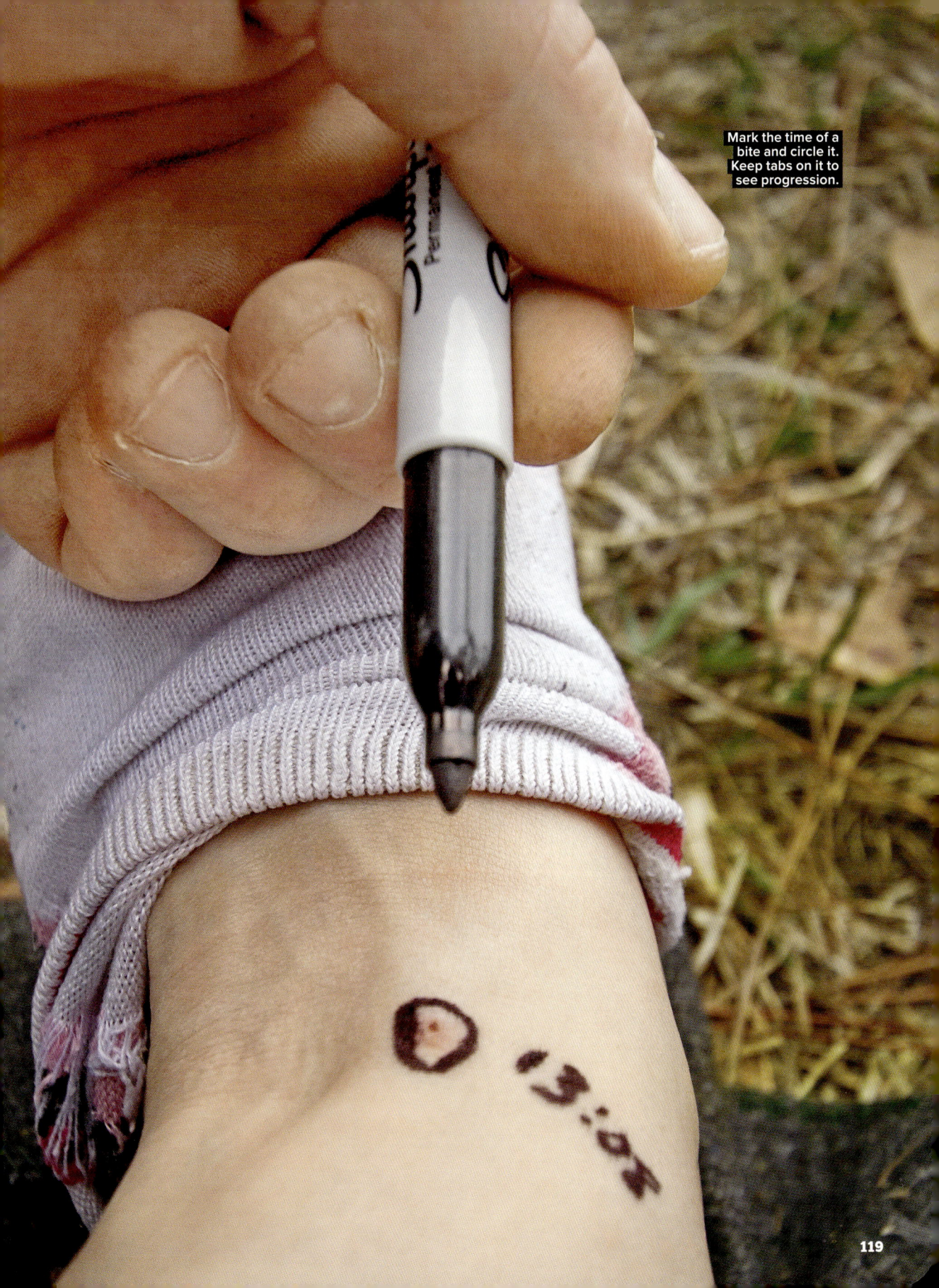

Mark the time of a bite and circle it. Keep tabs on it to see progression.

PLANNING

An emergency blanket is an important component of any first-aid kit.

ENVIRONMENTAL ISSUES

Beware if you start to notice signs of confusion among the members of your party during harsh weather. It is an early sign of hypothermia, or heat exhaustion. If your body's core temperature becomes too cold, or an extremity suffers frostbite from loss of blood circulation, passively rewarm yourself (or your companion) by adding dry clothing, getting under shelter and near a fire, and drinking a warm, noncaffeinated and nonalcoholic drink (a warm version of the electrolyte-replacement mix works well). Your Mylar emergency blanket can be used as an extra layer to contain body heat or for shelter in an emergency. Don't actively rewarm blistered, blue or waxy-looking skin by rubbing it. And only rewarm a frostbitten extremity when there is no longer a chance of refreezing it.

If the elements make you (or a companion) too hot, the most effective treatment is active cooling. Instant cold packs are essential; place them in the armpits, groin and neck to actively cool someone facing heat exhaustion or heat stroke. If you are close to a cool body of clean water, pour it over the head. Use electrolyte-replacement packets to rehydrate the body. If a person becomes so hot that they *stop* sweating, this is a sign of heat stroke and is a life-threatening emergency. After actively cooling the person as quickly as possible, they will need to be evacuated for further care.

—*Dane Boles*

CHECK IN FREQUENTLY WITH MEMBERS OF YOUR HIKING PARTY. OFTEN, YOU'LL NOTICE SIGNS OF HEAT EXHAUSTION, HEAT STROKE OR FROSTBITE BEFORE THE VICTIM DOES.

Dane Boles is an EMT in rural North Florida. In his free time, he enjoys hiking and paddling along the Southeastern U.S. and managing his homestead farm, goodfeatherfarms.com

VITAL SIGNS

Learning to obtain an accurate set of vital signs is an important first step in providing your own care in the backcountry. A wilderness first-aid class will teach these skills, while focusing on their application to medical emergencies in a remote setting. You can observe the following with nothing more than your own knowledge and a wristwatch: pulse; respiratory effort; skin color, temperature and moisture; capillary refill; and level of alertness. Oxygen saturation and body temperature can be noted using the pulse oximeter and thermometer in your medical kit.

Once you learn to take blood pressure, add a sphygmomanometer and stethoscope to your kit.

The normal ranges for various vital signs are listed below. The numbers are just guidelines; some people's "normal" ranges may be different from the ones listed. For instance, a very fit athlete may have a pulse that is normal for him/her, but that falls below the normal range shown here. Children, the elderly and those with certain medical conditions also deviate from these numbers. These ranges are assuming the person is an adult and "at rest."

Consider a wristwatch or smartwatch with a stopwatch feature to get accurate timed readings of vital stats.

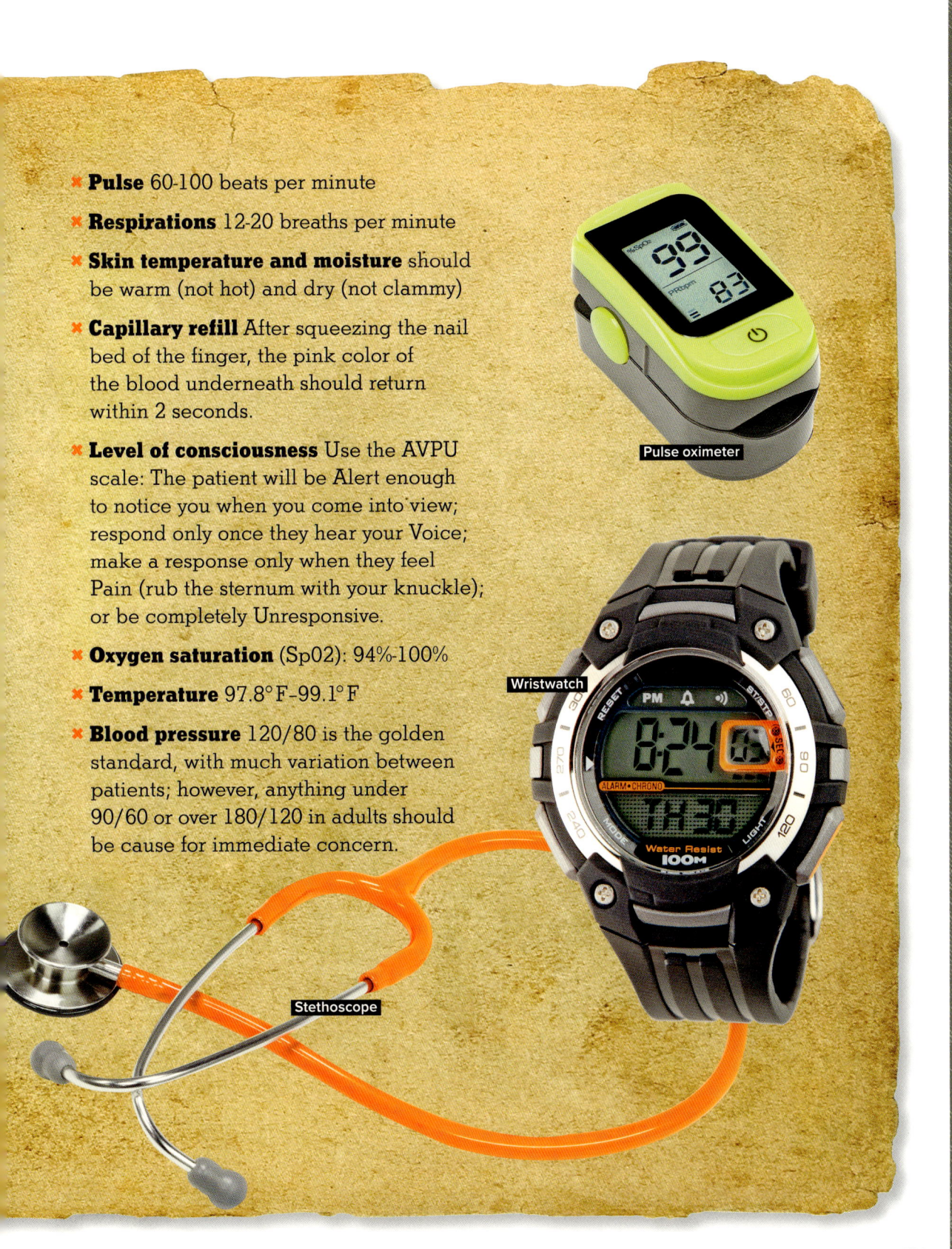

- **Pulse** 60-100 beats per minute
- **Respirations** 12-20 breaths per minute
- **Skin temperature and moisture** should be warm (not hot) and dry (not clammy)
- **Capillary refill** After squeezing the nail bed of the finger, the pink color of the blood underneath should return within 2 seconds.
- **Level of consciousness** Use the AVPU scale: The patient will be Alert enough to notice you when you come into view; respond only once they hear your Voice; make a response only when they feel Pain (rub the sternum with your knuckle); or be completely Unresponsive.
- **Oxygen saturation** (Sp02): 94%-100%
- **Temperature** 97.8°F-99.1°F
- **Blood pressure** 120/80 is the golden standard, with much variation between patients; however, anything under 90/60 or over 180/120 in adults should be cause for immediate concern.

Pulse oximeter

Wristwatch

Stethoscope

PLANNING

BASIC COMPACT FIRST-AID KIT

For a broad, yet compact, first-aid kit, consider this list a good foundation. You may add to it based on your own medical needs or as your medical knowledge advances. The goal is to have a small, easy-to-carry kit that will cover the most common maladies that occur in the backcountry, as well as contain the resources needed to stabilize serious injuries and illnesses until you can be extracted from the isolated environment. You can also keep a more extensive kit in your car or at a base camp. Consult with a doctor before taking any ingestible medications, and take extra precautions with giving medications to children, pregnant women, the elderly or those with medical complications or allergies.

- 2 pairs nitrile gloves
- SAM splint
- Ace bandage
- Triangular bandage with safety pins
- Wrapped tongue depressors
- Roll of Coban or Vet Wrap
- Roll of gauze
- Four 4-inch squares sterile gauze
- Roll of Transpore or cloth tape
- Basic Band-Aids (for cuts and blisters)
- 2 strips Vaseline petrolatum gauze or Curad Xeroform
- Tegaderm transparent adhesive film
- Mylar emergency blanket
- Instant cold packs
- Quality tweezers
- Trauma shears
- Thermometer
- AccuMed Pulse Oximeter
- Saline solution
- 6 alcohol, povidone-iodine, or BZK wipes
- Tube of triple-antibiotic ointment (w/o pain relief)
- 8 Motrin (ibuprofen)
- 8 Tylenol (acetaminophen)
- 6 Benadryl gel-caps (diphenhydramine)
- 4 Zantac (ranitidine)
- 4 Imodium (loperamide)
- Tin of Fisherman's Friend Original Extra Strong throat lozenges
- 12 sugar packets (1 teaspoon each)
- 16 salt packets (1/8 teaspoon each)
- Sharpie marker

FIRST AID

> SEEK OUT FIRST-AID TRAINING SO YOU KNOW HOW TO USE EVERYTHING IN YOUR KIT.

PLANNING

THE MOMENT YOU REALIZE THE SITUATION IS DIRE, STOP AND WEIGH YOUR OPTIONS.

A wilderness misadventure can be absolutely terrifying—but you *can* and *will* prevail, with the right mindset.

SURVIVAL PSYCHOLOGY

Keep your head to prevail over adverse conditions.

PLANNING

Stay aware of your surroundings when you're out exploring. If danger crops up, you'll be better prepared to deal with it.

THE SINGLE MOST IMPORTANT SURVIVAL TOOL YOU POSSESS LIES BETWEEN YOUR EARS. YOUR MIND IS FAR MORE POWERFUL THAN ANY GADGET OR BIT OF GEAR YOU COULD CARRY IN A PACK. IN FACT, YOU COULD POSSESS THE ENTIRE CONTENTS OF A HIGH-END SPORTING GOODS STORE AND STILL PERISH IF YOU CONVINCE YOURSELF THAT YOU AREN'T GOING TO MAKE IT.

However, it isn't always as simple as just deciding you're going to make it, though that is definitely a factor. There are several facets to the survival mindset.

FIGHT OR FLIGHT

Often, the first thing that happens when things go awry is the oft-discussed fight-or-flight response. Our bodies and minds prepare to either dive into combat or run like hell. See, our brains are wired for deep thinking when we have time for it, but when things get tough, we are capable of snap decisions. Sometimes we find ourselves taking action without even realizing we decided to do so.

In some cases, that's the desired response. We train and practice and drill so that we can react to danger and threats without having to think it through. If you're attacked by a mugger, the last thing you want is for your brain to seize up and try to

EVEN IF OUR BODY IS CAPABLE OF FINISHING THOSE LAST MILES ON THE TRAIL, IF THE BRAIN SAYS OTHERWISE, YOU'RE DEAD IN THE WATER.

PLANNING

A SMALL NOTEBOOK CAN BE A VALUABLE TOOL IN THE WILDERNESS.

If you have paper and pencil, writing down lists, goals and even just private thoughts can be helpful.

130 BACKWOODS SURVIVAL GUIDE

131

PLANNING

muddle through the different options you have available. Instead, you want to take fast and decisive action.

Fortunately, we can teach our brain to react in that way. We just need to take the time to do so. Learn how to use the fight-or-flight response in a positive manner, rather than just experiencing an adrenaline dump that makes you shiver and then gives you a nauseous stomach. Investing in serious study in a practical martial art can do wonders in this regard. Just knowing what to expect when you face danger can go a long way toward helping you to control your mind's reaction. The mind decides what the body will do, so if we're able to rewire the brain, we can react faster.

POSITIVE THINKING

Your attitude is crucial, because the body will follow the mind. Repeat something to yourself enough times and your brain will make it happen. Let's say you're hiking around a lake. You've been conditioning your body for the past several months and you're in decent shape, but during that last mile or two, you're really feeling it. You start thinking, "I can't do this, not today. I'm too tired,

> **WE NEED TO BE ABLE TO ROLL WITH THE CHANGES AND ADAPT OR ADJUST OUR PLANS TO FIT CHANGING CIRCUMSTANCES.**

my legs are rubber, it just isn't going to happen."

Guess what? You're probably right. Time and again, we've found that our minds can do some pretty interesting things, but not all of them are to our benefit. Even if our body is entirely capable of finishing those last couple of miles on that trail, if the brain tells the legs they can't take another step, you're dead in the water.

However, the reverse is also true. We can pull off some pretty incredible feats if we put our minds to it. When things aren't going your way, that's when you need to concentrate on the power of positive thinking. Repeat to yourself that you're going to succeed, that you've overcome worse situations or conditions, that you will make it home and see your loved ones again. Concentrate on that and you just may find that things are starting to look up.

While some folks seem to have an innate ability to always see the positive and land on their feet, regardless of the situation, many people don't have that luxury. Instead, any time you face some sort of negative experience, get into the habit of telling yourself that it is going to be OK, that it will all work out. Don't concentrate on the bad things that happen; instead, think about how strong you were when you were able to overcome them.

ANGER HELPS

For some people, anger can be a great motivator, if you keep it under control. Use the emotion—but don't let it use you. This is where ego can come into play. How dare the fates decide

PLANNING

Water, fire starters and first-aid supplies are just a few things you should have with you.

134 BACKWOODS SURVIVAL GUIDE

KEEPING A SMALL SURVIVAL KIT WITH YOU AT ALL TIMES CAN BE COMFORTING.

135

PLANNING

to test you! You're going to show them, and the world, just what happens when somebody messes with you.

However, the downside is that if you let anger run the show, you run the risk of making snap decisions that may not be in your favor. Further, a violent temper is rarely an asset, so keep your hands off your gear while you rant and rave, lest you end up breaking something or hurting yourself.

If you're with a partner or group, be very conscious of where you direct your anger. Alienating those who should be your allies is not a great idea.

PREPS LEND CONFIDENCE

An unseen and often unrealized bonus of having gear and supplies with you in a crisis is that it can give you a degree of peace of mind. For example, let's say you severely twist your ankle while you're on a solo hike in a remote area. The sun is going down fast and the temperature is dropping. Your cellphone has no signal and nobody is expecting to hear from you for at least a couple of days. No way around it: You're not going anywhere until morning at best.

This could be a fairly serious situation, and fear is a very natural response. But knowing you have emergency equipment in your pack, along with the skills needed to use them effectively, can give you confidence that you're going to see the sun come up again. This, in turn, plays into that positive thinking we mentioned earlier. Believe you're going to survive, that you're going to prevail, and you will!

ADAPTABILITY

One of the most important subsets of the survival mindset is being able to adapt to changes in your situation. Many times we get focused on a single track or plan and, when it doesn't pan out, we freeze up. We literally stop in our tracks because we don't know what to do. Think of it like going on a road trip. You've planned out the route and you're tooling along in your car when suddenly there's a detour sign. The road ahead is closed. Now what? It can be easy to make that decision when you're just out for a leisurely drive. Pick a direction and keep on trucking. Worst case scenario, you end up seeing part of the town or countryside you've never visited before.

But let's say this happens when you're running late for a job interview. Add in that pressure, and suddenly making decisions can be much more difficult. You could get locked into an endless loop of envisioning outcomes, with each of them seeming worse than the last.

Go a step further and instead of being late to an interview, you're facing what feels like the very real threat of death. Once you make a plan, you might be terrified to deviate from it even a little bit, in case doing so might lead to a very negative outcome.

Instead, we need to be able to roll with the changes and adapt or adjust our plans to fit. In a true survival situation, any plan of action needs to be fluid. Inevitably, the unexpected is going to come up at some point.

Go with the flow as best you can. Getting upset and stressed out because a plan didn't work is just a waste of energy. And in a survival situation, energy needs to be conserved to help you find another solution.

STRENGTH OF WILL

Strength of will is a single-minded determination that you will overcome any obstacles to make it home safely. While it sort of ties in with positive thinking, this is a more base-level response. Think of positive thinking as being your own cheerleader, whereas strength of will is the athlete competing on the field.

You must believe, at a molecular level, that nothing can stop you. This can be difficult, especially in prolonged situations. Depression, frustration, even guilt can all gnaw away at your resolve.

Never give up, never give in and you'll make it through.

MOTIVATIONAL TOOLS IN THE SURVIVAL KIT

One great way to foster a survival mindset in a truly awful situation is to find motivation to live. For some people, that can be difficult. What helps is to have with you an item or two that will not only bring psychological comfort, but provide motivation to survive, even thrive, and return home with a cool story to tell.

Perhaps a photo or two of your loved ones, kept in a sealed plastic bag to prevent damage, will give you something to concentrate on as you wait for rescue or try to decide what to do.

Another option might be a pocket-size version of the religious text of your preference. Prayer goes hand in hand with positive thinking. Anything that will motivate you to prevail is welcome. Use whatever it takes.

PLANNING

BUILDING SURVIVAL

Gearing up, one layer at a time.

Always bring essentials, but be careful not to weigh yourself down.

PLANNING

WE OFTEN HEAR ABOUT DRESSING IN LAYERS WHEN WE'RE VENTURING OUTDOORS. THE CONCEPT IS SOUND: IT ALLOWS US TO REGULATE OUR BODY TEMPERATURE BY SHEDDING GARMENTS WHEN WE GET TOO WARM, THEN BUNDLING BACK UP AS WE COOL DOWN. THERE IS ANOTHER APPLICATION OF THIS CONCEPT, THOUGH, AND THAT'S WITH YOUR EQUIPMENT AND GEAR.

When it comes to survival preparation, redundancy can be important. The catchphrase is, "Two is one, one is none." The idea is to have backups in case your primary tools and gear become unusable to you, through breakage, loss or other mishaps. Thinking in layers can make this concept simple to employ. Let's look at this from the inside out.

AGAINST THE SKIN

The first layer is what you keep on your body next to your skin. If you lose everything, even the very clothes on your back, you'd still theoretically have these items.

First on the list are things you could wear around your neck. A small knife would be a great idea, since having a cutting tool is very important. For fire, Wazoo Survival Gear makes a necklace that incorporates a little ferrocerium rod with a striker. A small but powerful whistle would make it easier to signal for help, should you end up in trouble.

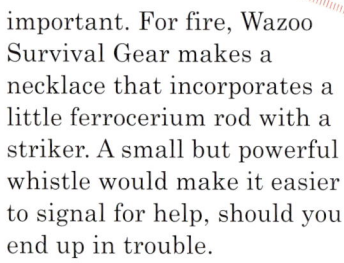

Another option would be a small compass on a lanyard. Remember, though, that a compass is only half of the navigation equation. You also need a map or some other means of determining exactly where you are and in which direction you need to travel to reach your destination.

There are two things to keep in mind with regard to neck-worn gear. First, having some sort of breakaway lanyard is ideal, just in case you somehow get hung up. Second, many people don't like to have very much weight hanging off their neck. Take a few test runs with your gear and decide which combination works best for you.

Another common option for wearing gear on the body is the paracord bracelet. When these bracelets first came on the scene, the idea was that they would provide you with several feet of cordage, should the need arise. Over the past several years, this concept has greatly expanded and now bracelets can be found that incorporate numerous other bits of gear, including fishing tackle, cutting tools, fire starters and more. There are several companies that specialize in these, such as Superesse Straps and Wazoo Survival Gear.

The caveat with these survival bracelets is that you need to know how to properly unknot them. If you have to cut the cordage apart, you'll limit your options as it shortens the available pieces of paracord.

POCKETS

Pockets probably started out as just loose folds in clothing that were secured in some way. Over time, people developed ways to add true pockets to clothing and the rest, as they say, is history. Pockets are where we can carry some of our primary-use gear, keeping it close at hand and easy to access. Of course, they range in size, capacity and placement.

Most of us tend to carry our EDC (every day carry) gear in our pockets. Typically, this includes:

- **Pocketknife**
- **Wallet**
- **Keys**
- **Flashlight**
- **Cellphone**
- **Lighter**
- **Handkerchief**
- **Tourniquet**

When you venture out into the field, you might add a hank of cordage, if you don't routinely carry it with you already. Other additions might include a compass, an emergency blanket and a signal mirror. A Fresnel lens can be used to focus sunlight to make fire, and also make it easier to see and remove splinters. Survival Resources carries a great one that fits right in your wallet.

STORING CORDAGE IN A POCKET

Want to know how to tie the world's strongest knot? Toss a pair of corded earbuds in your pocket and wait 30 seconds. But there is an easy way to carry a hank of cordage in your pocket where it will stay unknotted and easy to deploy. All you need is an old credit card or gift card. Cut a notch in one of the long sides of the card, up near a short side. Wedge one end of the cordage in that notch, then wrap the cordage around and around the card, working your way to the opposite end and back. When you've filled the card with as much cordage as you feel comfortable keeping in your pocket, cut the loose end and tuck it under a few of the loops.

Flashlight

Pocketknife

Cordage

PLANNING

A sturdy belt can carry a fair amount of gear.

BELT

A good belt will do more than just hold up your pants. It can be used to carry a number of useful items. First and foremost for a lot of people is a fixed blade knife. While there are many smaller knives that can be carried in the pocket, most people like to keep one on their belt. Depending on where you're going and what you'll be doing, a machete or small ax might also make sense to take along.

A multi-tool is another common belt-carry item. Most of them are a bit too bulky and heavy to be comfortable riding in a pocket.

Many manufacturers, such as Maxpedition and Vanquest, make a variety of belt pouches in different sizes. These help bridge the gap between pockets and actual packs or bags. As with everything else, though, personal preference and comfort are key. Some people like to have multiple pouches on their belt, filled with a wide range of gear and supplies. Others prefer one pouch at the most.

Play around with different configurations until you find one that suits you. This includes not just the size and location of the pouch (or pouches) but how much you

143

PLANNING

LOOK FOR PACKS AND BAGS THAT HAVE SEVERAL POCKETS INSIDE AND OUT. THEY'LL HELP YOU KEEP YOUR GEAR ORGANIZED.

carry in them. Some people find that they feel unbalanced if they have a heavy pouch riding on one hip without anything on the other side. Depending on the size of the pouch, you might find it interferes with your arm swing as you walk, but that's usually a simple adjustment.

PACKS AND BAGS

There are packs and bags in every size and shape you can imagine. One of the biggest struggles is to determine the correct size. In general, people tend to overestimate how large of a pack they need. The solution is to buy it last. Figure out what you need to carry first, then find one that will hold it all, with perhaps a tiny bit of additional space.

If you buy a pack that is too large, you'll still have a lot of empty space once you fill it with your gear. The tendency is to keep adding things until the pack is full, which means you'll eventually be carrying more weight than necessary.

Some people find that a sling bag, one that has just a single strap and is carried cross-body, is comfortable for short day hikes. Others don't like the bag bouncing on their hip as they walk.

Lastly, make sure the pack fits your body. Sporting goods and outdoors stores can often help you with fit. Remember that torso length—not overall height—is the key measurement. You can usually adjust the hip belt, shoulder straps, load-lifter straps and sternum strap to find your perfect fit. The majority of the load should rest on your hips.

Sling bag

Layering gear will spread the weight instead of having it all on your back.

145

146 BACKWOODS SURVIVAL GUIDE

CHAPTER 4

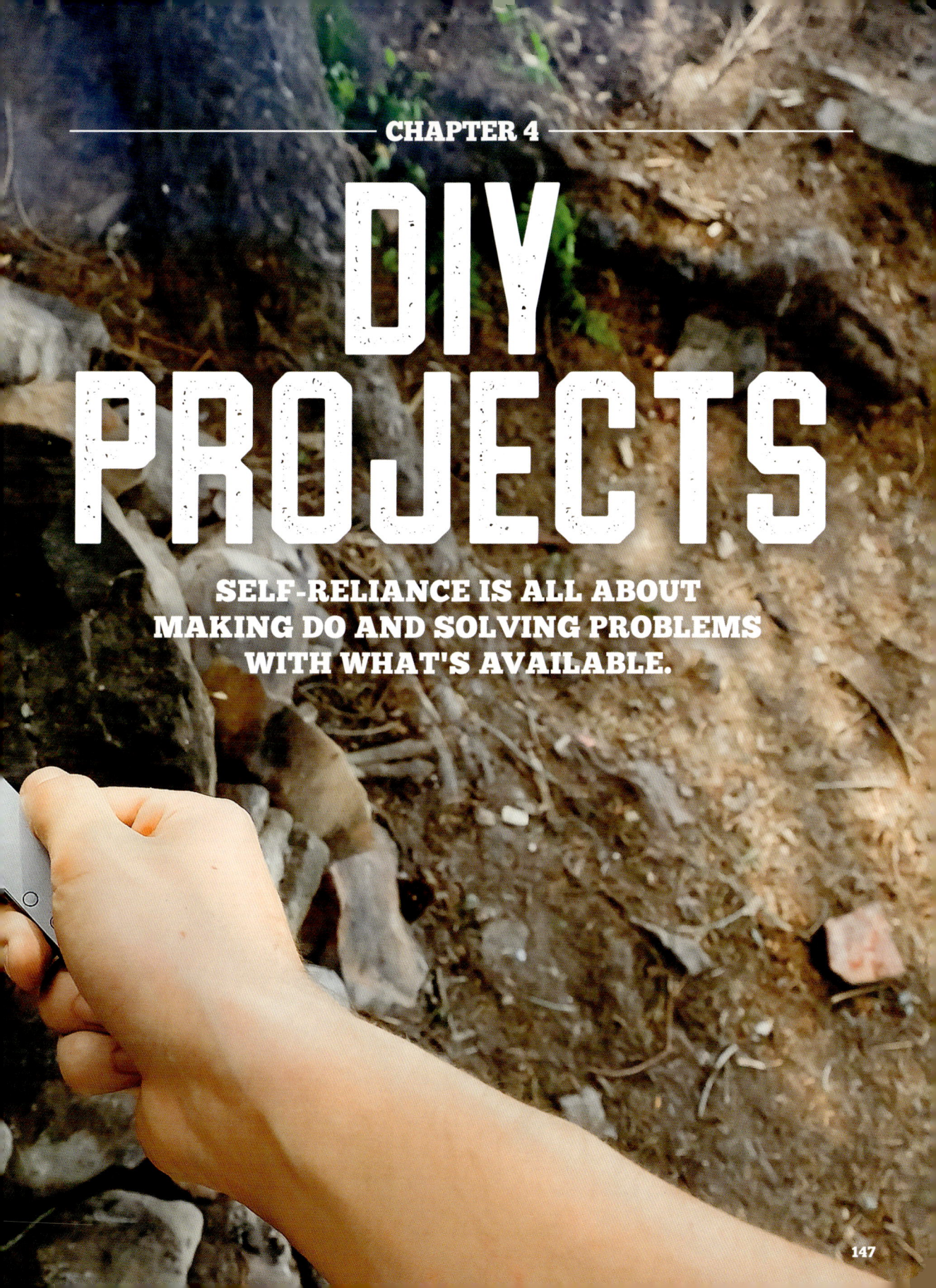

DIY PROJECTS

SELF-RELIANCE IS ALL ABOUT MAKING DO AND SOLVING PROBLEMS WITH WHAT'S AVAILABLE.

DIY PROJECTS

MAKE YOUR OWN OILCLOTH TARP

Some gear is very expensive. With this DIY project, you can save a pretty penny.

A waterproof tarp is an invaluable part of your gear, especially when the weather turns bad.

DIY PROJECTS

WHEN BUYING OUTDOOR GEAR, YOU SHOULD BUY THE BEST YOU CAN AFFORD. BUT IF THE HIGH PRICE TAG OF COMMERCIALLY MADE TARPS BRINGS TEARS TO YOUR EYES, MAKE YOUR OWN USING SUPPLIES YOU MOST LIKELY HAVE ON HAND. I MADE MINE FOUR YEARS AGO AFTER WATCHING WILLIAM COLLINS' FOUR-PART TUTORIAL ON YOUTUBE. HERE'S WHAT YOU NEED TO KNOW.

WHAT YOU'LL NEED

- **100 percent cotton flat bedsheet** (350+ thread-count Egyptian cotton works well)
- **½-inch-wide oil-lamp wick** (for tie-outs)
- **Boiled linseed oil**
- **Odorless mineral spirits**
- **Dye** in your desired color (optional)
- **Needle and thread** or sewing machine
- **Containers and pots** (don't use the family's good pots!)
- **Rubber gloves**

Mix these two in a 1:1 ratio.

151

DIY PROJECTS

Tarps will dry much more quickly on a dry day.

YOU CAN PICK UP A SHEET FROM GOODWILL OR ANOTHER THRIFT STORE RATHER THAN USE ONE FROM YOUR LINEN CLOSET.

HOW TO MAKE

1 Whether you buy a new sheet or steal one from the linen closet, wash it in cold water and dry on high heat to shrink the cotton fibers as much as possible.

2 For tie-outs, sew ½- x 6-inch pieces of lamp wick on the sheet edges at 2-foot intervals, starting at the corners. I hand-stitched them with upholstery thread. I used a 8.5- x 9-foot king-size sheet and attached three additional loops down the center line to give additional options for different tarp configurations.

Hickory nuts (with black walnuts to be added) for the dye mixture

A long, slow boil to extract pigments from the nut husks

3 If the color of your sheet is to your liking, skip to step 9. If not, dye your sheet. You can use natural materials for your dye. Green hickory nuts and/or black walnuts are two natural dyeing agents to consider. (If you can't wait for the nuts to drop, pick up some RIT dye from the store, the stuff used to make funky tie-dye T-shirts.)

4 If you're using purchased dye, follow the package instructions to dye your sheet. If you're going the natural route, in a large pot, place enough nuts to cover the bottom. (If you want to crush or cut the husks off the nuts first, wear heavy-duty gloves to avoid staining your hands a lovely shade of brown; this is a messy matter.)

5 Fill the pot half to three-quarters full of water and bring to a boil on an outside heat source. Maintain a slow, steady boil for at least an hour. The longer you boil the husks, the darker the dye becomes. About an hour and a half of boiling produced the earth tone I was looking for. It's wise to test the dye on scrap fabric before dunking your entire sheet.

DIY PROJECTS

6 Strain the dye liquid into a 5-gallon bucket. An old window screen or T-shirt secured over your collection bucket works fine as a sieve.

7 Submerge your sheet into the dye bucket for 24 hours. I placed a 25-pound barbell on a dinner plate as a weight. This resulted in crimping the sheet, which created slightly darker dye lines on the finished product. I liked the way these lines created a broken pattern in the color scheme.

8 The next day, wring excess liquid from the sheet and hang it to air dry. Our double clothesline was perfect for the task. When dry, place it in the washing machine and wash it with detergent in cold water. Cold water sets the dye in the fabric. No, it won't stain the washing drum. Dry it again on high in the clothes dryer.

9 To waterproof a king-size sheet, I mixed three Solo cups each of boiled linseed oil and odorless mineral spirits in a 5-gallon bucket. Wearing heavy rubber dishwashing gloves, stir in the sheet until fully saturated with the concoction.

10 Wring the excess solution out of the sheet. Keep the extra

Stirring the sheet into the dye for full coverage

USING TWO CLOTHESLINES LIKE THIS TO DRY THE TARP MAY LEAVE MARKS.

Drying the oilcloth may take several days.

Two lines left from hanging on the double clothesline

Testing the tarp once the waterproofing has fully cured

waterproofing liquid in a sealed container for future projects. Hang the sheet to air dry. If you use a double clothesline like I did, visible lines may form on your tarp where it contacted the clothesline. To prevent this, hang your sheet to dry vertically. Clotheslines aren't typically tall enough to hang a sheet without folding. I finished the drying process by hanging the sheet from shed rafters.

Drying time depends on humidity and temperature. With dry weather, the tarp should cure in about 48 hours. The smell of boiled linseed oil lingered in my tarp for a week or so in our humid Georgia climate.

11 Once your tarp is dry to the touch, grab a garden hose and give it a simulated rain shower. Even using the hose on the jet spray setting, I found the inside of the tarp bone-dry.

12 My tarp weighs just over 3 pounds. Keep in mind that you're dealing with a bedsheet, not a heavy-duty canvas tarp. Too much tension on tie-outs can cause tears. With normal use and care, your tarp should offer many years of dependable use in the woods or homestead.

—*Todd Walker*

155

DIY PROJECTS

Patience is a virtue in fire-making. Sometimes you'll need to gently coax that ember into a flame.

FEW SITUATIONS ARE MADE WORSE WITH THE ADDITION OF A WARM CAMPFIRE.

LIGHT IT UP AND LET IT BURN

A combustion kit is a survival essential.

DIY PROJECTS

IN A TRUE LIFE-OR-DEATH SURVIVAL SITUATION, STRIKING SPARKS AND COAXING THEM INTO A FULL-FLEDGED FLAME CAN HELP TO GIVE YOU A SENSE OF CONTROL OVER WHAT'S HAPPENING. SURVIVAL IS JUST AS MUCH MENTAL AS IT IS PHYSICAL, SO ANYTHING THAT CAN GIVE YOU AN EDGE, THAT CAN BOLSTER YOUR SELF-CONFIDENCE, IS WELCOME.

Fire requires three basic ingredients. There must be fuel, oxygen and heat. This is often represented in a triangle symbol, with each of those elements forming a side. Remove any one of them and the fire dies. Smothering a flame with a blanket removes the oxygen. Pouring water on it cools the fuel below the point of combustion. If it runs out of fuel, it sputters out.

When you assemble a fire kit to carry in your pack, do so by focusing on making sure you have accounted for all three sides of the combustion triangle.

FUEL

Obviously you're not going to be packing sticks and logs in your kit. In this instance, fuel refers to tinder. The focus is on having material that is easy to light and that burns long enough to help get the rest of the fire lit. There are three basic types of tinder:

Natural tinder includes things like birch bark, cattail fluff and fatwood. These materials and others like them can be readily found in many wilderness areas. Items like bark should be torn and fluffed up to create as much surface area as possible. Fatwood should be scraped to

Fatwood should be scraped to create a small pile of dust.

Whenever possible, use these sorts of natural tinder rather than what you have packed in your fire kit. Reserve your supply for the times when you're unable to find a local source of tinder.

The next type of tinder is homemade. These are items that you pack up yourself from materials you find around the house. Dryer lint is a common one, and it can work well. But if most of your wardrobe consists of man-made fabrics like polyester blends, you might find the lint in your dryer doesn't burn very well. Lint from cotton fabrics works the best. Cotton balls also work great, especially if you mix them with petroleum jelly.

Most homemade tinder concoctions are variations on that. You can try dryer lint or cotton balls mixed with one or more other ingredients, such as sawdust, bits of cardboard and such, then covered in petroleum jelly. Store the tinder in resealable plastic bags to avoid staining other items in your pack.

The third category of tinder consists of items that are store-bought. There are many brand-name products that work outstandingly well when it comes to getting a fire lit quickly. Solkoa Fastfire is one of the best on the market. It consists of a cube of white material that can be shaved or crumbled. It lights instantly with spark or flame, and burns at about 1,300°F.

Another excellent commercially produced tinder product is Instafire. It is a granular substance that is packed in pouches. Pour out a small pile, light it and it burns hot for several minutes. There are also various "tinder tab" products that you can find at just about any sporting goods store. These little fiber bundles burn well, but you have to remember to pull them apart and fluff them up before lighting.

Keep a couple of different tinder options in your kit. If one type doesn't seem to be working well in your situation, try another.

Tinder is anything that is dry, fluffy and easily lit.

DIY PROJECTS

HEAT

When you start a fire, what you do is create a chemical reaction by introducing a high amount of heat to the tinder, causing it to ignite. There are numerous options for tools designed to accomplish this, with the humble disposable cigarette lighter being at the top of the list. Virtually every survival instructor out there, no matter how experienced and skilled they are with primitive fire-making, will carry a Bic lighter in their pocket just in case.

As any smoker knows, disposable lighters don't work well in cold conditions. This problem can often be solved by warming the lighter in a tight fist for several seconds or by carrying it in a pocket close to your skin. However, even if it won't light, the sparks it generates can still be used on most forms of tinder.

Strike-anywhere matches have a home in many survival kits. I wouldn't suggest them as a primary fire starter because they are much more disposable than other options—meaning, once you've lit a match, you can't use it again. But they can serve as a backup if you keep them in a container that's waterproof.

A ferrocerium rod is the preferred tool for many preppers if a disposable lighter isn't available.

DIY PROJECTS

The venerable ferrocerium rod is a fixture in most fire kits and for good reason. It works amazingly well. It is sometimes sold under names like spark rod or flint rod (despite not being made of flint). The concept is simple: Scraping the rod with a sharp edge causes bits of the rod to shave off and ignite from the friction, turning into sparks that rain down onto your tinder. The ferro rod works in any weather conditions, making it an excellent addition to the fire-making toolbox.

A Fresnel lens is a magnifying lens that can focus the sun's rays to a small point, igniting the tinder. While this tool isn't of much use at night, it is small and light enough to be carried in a wallet as a backup fire-starting method.

While the hope is that every fire you'll ever need to light can be started with the flick of a disposable lighter, that may not be realistic in all situations. Have multiple fire starters in your kit and scattered among your pockets just in case.

OXYGEN

If you're able to breathe where you're building the fire, then odds are there's enough oxygen, right? Yes and no. There's plenty of oxygen in the air, yes, but it is a matter of making sure the air is reaching the fire.

One of the most common mistakes I see people make when it comes to building a fire is smothering it. You have to let it breathe. Leave room for plenty of air flow when constructing the fire lay. Don't rush it and add too much fuel too quickly. Take it slow and coax the fire to life with an extremely gentle touch.

> **A COMMON MISTAKE IS TO SMOTHER THE FIRE. YOU HAVE TO LEAVE ROOM FOR AIR FLOW IN ORDER TO LET IT BREATHE.**

PRIMITIVE FIRE-MAKING METHODS

Long before the advent of disposable lighters and store-bought tinder, mankind was making fire using bow drills and other primitive methods. As a general rule, these fire-making techniques rely upon generating enough friction to cause an ember to form. This little glowing jewel is gently transferred to the tinder bundle and slowly nursed into flame.

Primitive skills are awesome additions to the toolbox. They are both fun and functional. However, eschewing all modern tools in favor of these skills in a true survival situation probably isn't the best idea. Even the very best fire-makers fail from time to time with bow drills and other such tools. Always have multiple means to accomplish basic survival tasks like making a fire.

A BOW DRILL IS AN EXCELLENT FIRE STARTER AND WILL WARM YOU UP AS YOU USE IT!

Primitive fire-making skills are great to learn and practice, but don't forget to toss a disposable lighter into your pocket just in case.

DIY PROJECTS

KNOT IMPORTANCE

Tie up loose ends with these six must-know knots!

CORDAGE IS, WITHOUT A DOUBT, ONE OF THE TOP COMPONENTS OF MOST BUG OUT BAGS. FROM PARACORD TO FISHING LINE TO ALL-PURPOSE ROPE, THE NEED FOR EXTRA-STRONG CORDAGE IS CRUCIAL FOR SHELTER, CATCHING FOOD, SETTING UP A RAIN-CATCH, AND A MYRIAD OF OTHER SURVIVAL USES.

But as with the weakest link in a chain, cordage is only as strong as its attachment point, and that's where specialized knots come into play.

Whether needing an easily removable knot, joining two shorter pieces of cordage together, or even setting up loops across your strand, knowing how to create some of the most basic, yet useful, knots when out "in the field" is, without a doubt, an indispensable survival skill.

> **CORDAGE AND KNOT SKILLS ARE ESSENTIAL FOR THE SURVIVALIST.**

Knot tying can be practiced anywhere.

DIY PROJECTS

COW HITCH KNOT

The cow hitch (a member of the overall Hitch Knot group) is a very simple knot used to attach cordage to an object. This type of attachment dates back approximately two centuries, perhaps even earlier. It's almost a guarantee that most people have used it as a simple, quick way of securing items to cordage (even if they didn't know the name of the knot they were using), when adding zipper pulls to a jacket or gear bag, securing a corner ring of a tent, or making a semi-secure strap around the wrist when holding a flashlight or other electronic gear. One distinct characteristic that makes it very easy to create is that it can be tied either with the end of the cordage or by using the bight itself. The cow hitch is also known as the lark's head, in addition to having numerous variations based upon an individual's needs.

1 Slide one end of your cordage through a ring. **2** Bring it down and across your initial line. **3** Guide it up through the ring and move it down through the rounded hanging loop. **4** Continue to pull through and tighten as desired.

DIY PROJECTS

ALPINE BUTTERFLY KNOT

The alpine butterfly knot's main function is to create a loop or loops across a length of cordage. The usefulness of this type of knot is that no access is needed from either end of the rope to create it. This makes it incredibly valuable during climbing, where carabiners need to be quickly secured; when a rope or cord must be shortened to reduce sag; and even when a damaged piece of rope needs to be isolated, as to not reduce the integrity of the entire line. Major advantages to adding this knot to your toolbox is that it can be tied without difficulty when wearing gloves; it is relatively easy to untie; and it adds numerous secure points when secondary ropes are not readily available. Other names for this knot include lineman's loop, butterfly knot and lineman's rider.

1 Create a figure eight within any length of your cordage. **2** Bring the top circle of the "eight" downward below the cord run. **3** Maneuver the lower loop behind the bulk of cordage and up through the center "triangle." **4** Pull tightly to create a solid loop.

DIY PROJECTS

BLOOD KNOT

Nearly all bug out bags or emergency kits have some type of fishing gear, although most are limited in how many hooks or how much line is included. This means every inch of monofilament line is precious—and that's where the blood knot proves its worth. This knot, sometimes referred to as a barrel knot, is primarily used to join broken fishing lines together with minimal loss of tensile strength. Knowing how to tie this type of knot is crucial when depending upon the sea or a nearby freshwater outlet for your next meal. It not only tightly joins the two pieces of line, but it does so at a very effective rate, hovering around 80 percent. The main drawback to this type of knot is that it requires great dexterity to tie it—and in rough outdoor conditions, this could be a problem.

1 Create an intersection of two lengths of cordage. 2 Wrap each piece around the other five times. 3 Bring the end of one strand through the intersected opening. 4 Bring the end of the other strand through the intersected opening. 5 Pull both ends tightly. 6 Cut off any remaining cordage from loose ends.

DIY PROJECTS

STRANGLE KNOT

With a distinctive—but somewhat ghoulish—name, this knot is a simple binding knot. Useful for tying up sacks or other similar bags, the relative ease of tying this knot is only surpassed by its strength, once it tightens down on itself. This characteristic makes it ideal for preventing the fraying of rope or other cordage. Although it is less secure than its cousin, the constrictor, most people who use this binding like that it lays flat once it is tightened from both ends. As time passes, the security of the binding will only increase, forming a highly stable connection. The strangle knot is also useful when plaiting or braiding cordage; you can use the knot to attach the cordage lengths to a branch and let them hang down for braiding.

1 Position the end of a piece of cordage over a piece of wood and bring the end upward. 2 Drop the end down and then across your initial piece strand. 3 Pass the end through between the loops already wrapped around the stick. 4 Finally, pull and tighten both ends.

FIGURE EIGHT LOOP

While it's the go-to knot used by climbers everywhere, the figure eight loop is essential for survivalists and outdoorsmen for innumerable purposes. This knot is very strong and secure when tied, and the loop won't slip under any conditions, which makes it useful for grabbing by hand or stepping into with your foot. There are two ways that this knot can be tied: using double line, or with the "figure eight follow-through." The double-line method is faster, but it can't be used when tying to a fixed object. If you're just creating the loop, this way is lightning-fast; the follow-through method of tying takes a bit more effort and time, but offers greater versatility for a variety of survival and everyday needs. A back-up knot using the tag end is often used to give this already strong knot an even more reliable hold.

1 Double any desired length of rope or cordage. 2 Form the end portion into a circle and hold it with your hand. 3 Slip the end loop through the double-corded circle. 4 Pull for a slip-free loop.

DIY PROJECTS

FISHERMAN'S BEND KNOT

Ideal for joining two pieces of cordage into one, the fisherman's bend is a simple-to-learn knot that comes in very handy when rope or line is not readily available, such as during a survival scenario, and you need to make do with what's nearby. Although "slippery" line, such as monofilament, may slide initially, it only takes a few more turns of the overhead knot to increase its strength and ensure a firm hold. This type of knot is widely used in necklaces, mainly those constructed of leather cordage, offering a simple way to adjust the size of the circumference to suit a person's needs. This knot is also known as an English knot, waterman's knot and halibut knot.

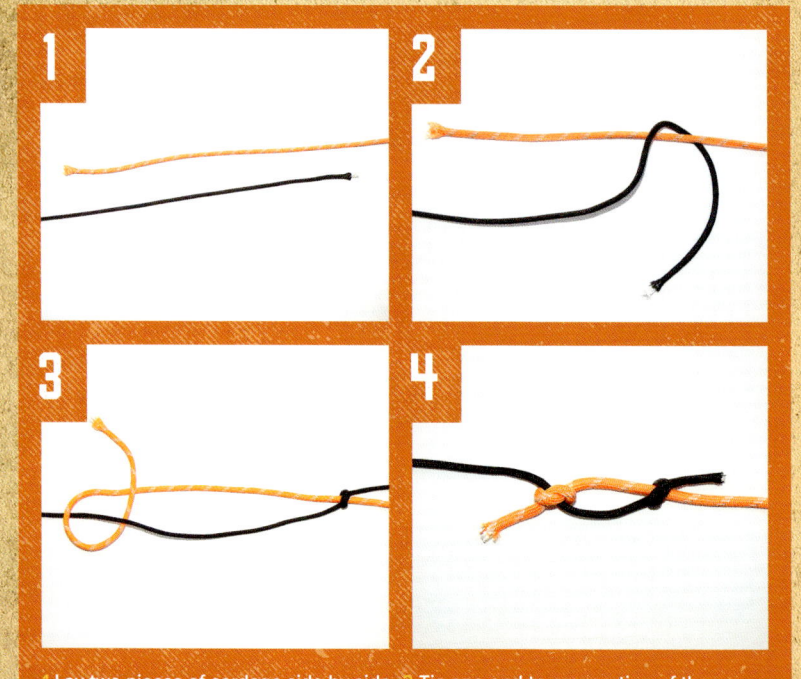

1 Lay two pieces of cordage side by side. **2** Tie one end to any portion of the other piece. **3** Repeat for the other length and tighten both knots. **4** Adjust the desired length by pulling both knots either apart or toward one another.

TIE A KNOT...AND WEAKEN YOUR ROPE!

Knots have many functions and are useful in numerous circumstances, both in survival situations and during regular daily life. But beware: Knots have a bad side. They have an innate ability to reduce a rope's strength and possibly cause severe injury or even death.

This often-overlooked effect is caused by tension produced on the outside of the bent line when a knot is formed, as well as compression on the inside. The stress upon the rope is increased, and inversely, the strength of the rope is decreased. It's a dual causality; while the outside bend is under higher tension, the inside of the loop fibers bunch up and fail to offer their normal amount of strength, as they do when the strand is in its straight, or unknotted, form.

Although some assume a generality of 50 percent strength decrease once a knot has been applied, this type of thinking can cause disaster if one's life hangs in the balance. The truth is that different knots on different materials produce varied results—and anyone who puts their life on the line needs to do their homework concerning rope strength, knots and the relationship they have with each other. It may not only save them from losing their load, but may also prevent them from losing their life!

DIY PROJECTS

You don't need to go out and purchase a ton of fishing tackle. Just the basics are enough to get you started.

176 BACKWOODS SURVIVAL GUIDE

REEL 'EM IN!

A hook and line is all you need to secure dinner.

FANCY RODS AND REELS ARE FUN, BUT THEY CAN BE EXPENSIVE. START SMALL.

DIY PROJECTS

A MAJOR FACTOR IN SURVIVAL IS ENERGY CONSERVATION. YOU SHOULD TRY TO AVOID EXPENDING MORE ENERGY ON AN ACTIVITY THAN YOU'RE GOING TO GET OUT OF IT. THIS IS PARTICULARLY TRUE WHEN IT COMES TO FOOD ACQUISITION. SPENDING HOURS TRACKING GAME IN HOPES OF GETTING THAT ONE GOOD SHOT IS A GAMBLE THAT YOU PROBABLY DON'T WANT TO MAKE.

Trapping is certainly a possibility if you possess the requisite knowledge and skills. However, if you think you'll be able to just set up a couple of snares and come back in an hour to pick up your meal, you're setting yourself up for failure.

Most of us have gone fishing at least a few times in our lives. And while we might not have landed a world-record bass, a few bluegills or perch can fill a belly just the same. As a general rule, you'll expend far less energy fishing than you will just with about any other activity related to obtaining sustenance. Putting together a small fishing kit will help ensure you have the basic gear you'll need to land dinner.

LINE

If there's one truly essential component in the fishing kit, it is the line. While you could use a shoelace or something similar, having a supply of actual fishing line makes everything so much easier. All of the other bits of gear needed could be improvised or scavenged, though again, the idea here is to have what you need when you need it.

Braided fishing line is a far better choice than monofilament and it is definitely worth the additional cost. Monofilament line has what is called memory, which means that after it has been stored all rolled up, it wants to stay spooled rather than straighten out. Braided line doesn't have this issue.

One of the easiest ways I've found to store line in the kit is to use sewing bobbins. You can store several dozen yards of line on a bobbin and have it take up very little space in the kit. As a bonus, the bobbin keeps the line from getting tangled.

HOOKS

A key thing to remember about hooks is that you can catch big fish with a small hook, but it is nearly impossible to catch small fish with a big hook. It is simple mechanics. If the hook is too big for the fish's mouth, no matter how tasty the bait is, the fish will live to swim another day.

Hooks can be lost rather easily, such as if the fish

swallows it or the line gets wrapped up underwater. Therefore, you'll want a good number of hooks in the kit—at least two dozen. Fortunately, hooks are cheap.

A small plastic envelope is one storage option for the hooks. Depending on the overall size of the kit, an old 35mm film canister can also serve quite well.

SWIVELS

The purpose of a fishing swivel is to keep the line from tangling as you retrieve the fish. However, using them causes a bit of a weak link in the chain, and landing big fish can be problematic. That said, odds are you'll be seeing many more panfish and the like than you will monster-sized largemouth bass.

Toss several swivels into a small plastic bag and you'll be good to go.

SINKERS

Without adding some weight to the end of the line, the bait might just float on the water's surface rather than sinking down to where the fish are waiting. Split-shot sinkers are very easy to use as you can clip them on to the line or take them off as needed. They also come in a range of sizes.

Sinkers

BOBBERS

A bobber, or float, isn't absolutely necessary most of the time when you're fishing, but at a minimum it will make it easier to see where your line enters the water. There are several options to consider for the floats. Store-bought bobbers come in different sizes, styles and colors. They are also relatively inexpensive.

There are a few reasons a float is desirable. First, it will help keep the bait suspended at a specific depth. Second, by watching the bobber, you'll get a heads-up that something is interested in your bait.

If your kit is too small for traditional bobbers, improvise. Foam earplugs work very well as floats. Another option is to carry small uninflated balloons in the kit.

Of course, you could always just use a small twig or something similar.

DIY PROJECTS

TROTLINES

Setting out a trotline is an excellent way to increase the odds of success when fishing. It is also illegal in most areas, but I'd hazard to guess that if you're in a situation where you're considering setting one out, you'd welcome seeing someone from the Department of Natural Resources pull up.

A trotline is simply a series of baited hooks suspended from a length of cordage. The idea is to catch several fish, rather than just one at a time. Tie one end of the paracord or other cordage to a tree or rock on shore. Then at regular intervals on the cordage, attach short lines with hooks. Bait the hooks, then run the cordage into the water in a straight line. Attach the free end to a stationary object on the opposite side, assuming this is a narrow stream.

Or you can find a large float, such as an old milk jug, and tie your cordage to that, then weigh it down with some sort of anchor.

With the right tools and a little patience, dinner can be had.

DIY PROJECTS

ARTIFICIAL BAIT

Many fishing kits contain a number of spinners, rubber worms and other artificial bait options. Stock a small variety of them in your DIY kit. However, you should always try to find live bait in the area when you're ready to fish. Look under rocks and logs for bugs and worms. When using worms, use small bits at a time, rather than the entire worm at once. This prevents fish from just nibbling the bait away, wasting your resources.

BLADE

Personally, I always lean toward adding a sharp knife to just about any kit, including one designed for fishing. You'll need to be able to cut and trim line, of course, and if you manage to catch something, you'll need something to clean the fish and prepare it for the fire.

A small folding knife will be sufficient, though there are several small neck knives on the market that could fit into a fishing kit if you'd rather go that route.

CONTAINER

Gather your desired supplies together first, then choose a container into which they will all fit. Too often, if we select the container first, we either end up with not enough space or way too much.

The container should be sturdy as well as waterproof. The venerable Altoids tin is a popular choice. It isn't waterproof on its own, but with the addition of a wide rubber band around the edge, it'll do just fine. This should be large enough to carry all of the basics.

FISHING TIPS

In just a single article, it would be impossible to even scratch the surface when it comes to fishing techniques, which will vary depending on the area you're in and the type of fish that populate that area. However, here are a few pointers:

Fish tend to be most active in the mornings and evenings. Those are the times when you're most likely to catch them.

Try different baits. If you aren't having any luck with worms, try bugs or lures.

Set the hook quickly but not too forcefully. When you feel a bite, you'll want to give the line a jerk so the hook digs in. If you pull too hard, you could rip the hook out of the fish's mouth.

A KEY THING TO REMEMBER ABOUT HOOKS IS THAT YOU CAN CATCH BIG FISH WITH A SMALL HOOK, BUT THE REVERSE ISN'T TRUE.

Treble hook

Fishing before the sun rises is often the best way to have a successful haul.

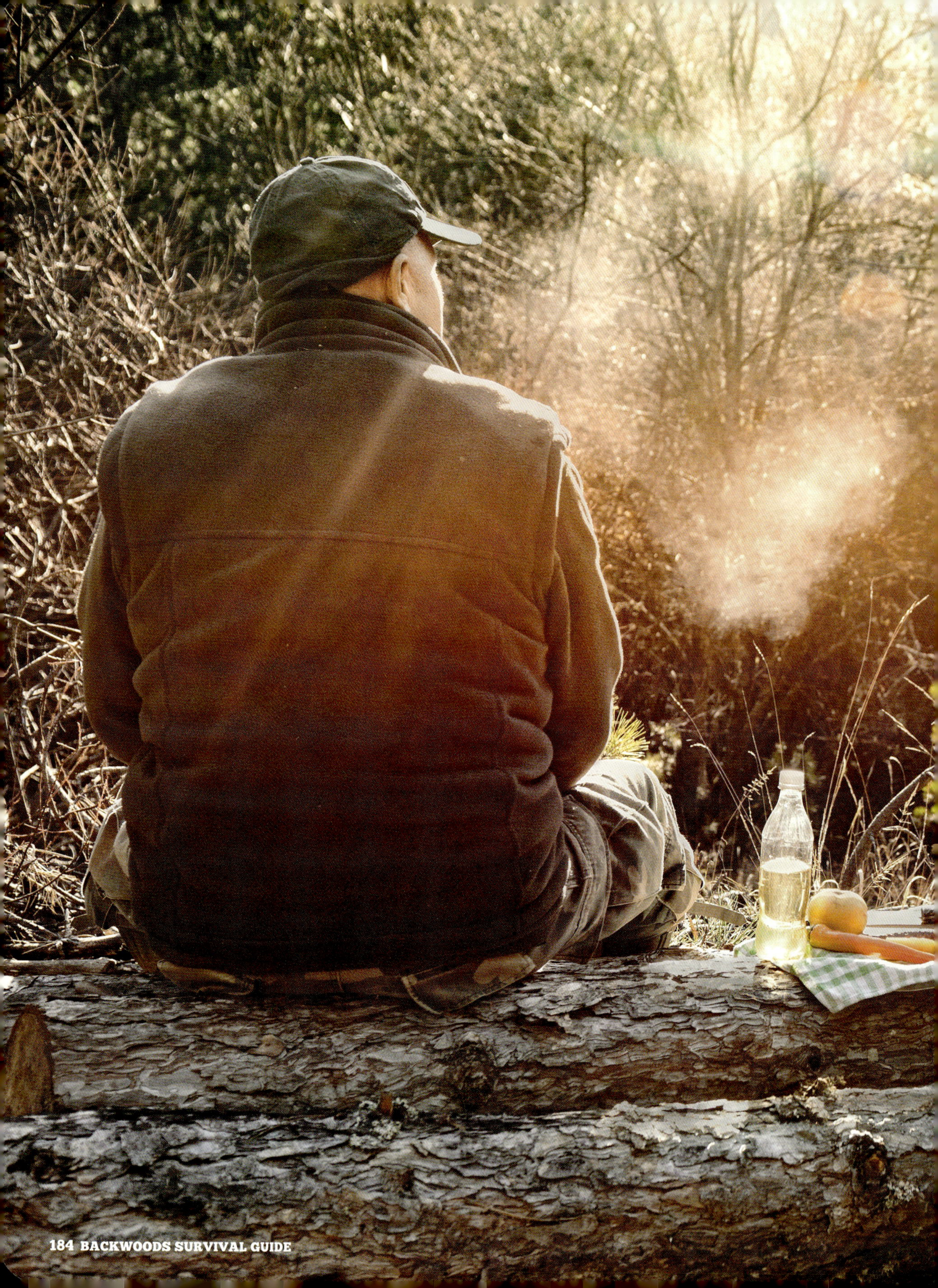

Enjoy the solitude of the wilderness—but always be prepared before you head out.

INDEX

A
Active cooling/rewarming, 121
Adaptability, 136
Airflow
    for fire production, 162
    for food preservation, 95
Aloe, 13, 18–19
Alpine butterfly knot, 168–169
Aluminum foil footprint, 106
Anger, as motivator, 133, 136
AVPU scale, 123
Awareness of surroundings, 129

B
Backpacks
    alternatives to, 138–145
    organizing gear in, 144
    for women, 41–44
Backup charger, 111
Bags, for carrying gear, 144
Bait, for fishing, 182
Balance, walking stick for, 53–55
Baldric rigs, 41–44
Beans, 68
Belts
    for carrying gear, 142–144
    cross-body, for women, 41–44
Berries, 73
Bindle, 57
Bites and stings
    first aid for, 118
    marking time of, 118, 119
Blanket. See Emergency blanket
Bleeding, controlling, 116
Blood knot, 170–171
Blood pressure, normal range, 123
Bobbers, fishing, 179
Bow drill, 162
Bracelets, gear in, 140–141
Breakaway lanyards, 140
Broccoli, 72
Burns, first aid for, 116

Bushcraft, 7, 8, 10–61
    gatherings/online groups, 46–47
    modifications for women, 38–49

C
Camera stand, 57
Canning, as food preservation method, 96–97
Capillary refill, 123
Carrots, 68
Cellphone, 111
Clothing, what to select, 40–41
Communicating with others, about travel plans, 106
Compass, 105, 140
Confidence, preparation providing, 136
Consciousness, level of, 123
Container, fishing tackle, 182
Cooling, 121
Cordage
    knot-tying guide, 164–175
    rope strength and, 175
    storing in pocket, 141
    in survival kit, 82
    for survival shelter construction, 33
    when hiking, 112
Corn, 73
Cow hitch knot, 166–167
Crops for survival garden, 68–73
Cross-body bags/belts, 41–44, 144

D
Debris hut, 36–37
Defense, walking stick for, 61
Dehydrating, as food preservation method, 92, 95
Diarrhea, 118
Digging holes, walking stick for, 57, 60
Disinfection. See Water disinfection
Disposable lighter, 160
DIY projects, 7, 8, 146–183
    combustion kit, 156–163
    knot-tying guide, 164–175
    oilcloth tarp, 148–155
Dressing in layers, clothing and gear, 138–145

E

Emergency blanket
   for survival shelter, 33
   for survival shelter construction, 33
   when hiking, 112, 120–121
Environmental issues, first aid and, 121

F

Ferrocerium rod, 112, 140, 161–162
Fight-or-flight response, 128, 133
Figure eight loop knot, 173
Filtration. See Water filter/filtration
Fire kit, 33, 112, 134, 140
Fire-making methods, 156–163
First aid, 114–125
   training in, 125
First-aid kit, contents of, 134
   basic, 124–125
Fisherman's bend knot, 174
Fishing
   tackle for, 178–179, 182
   tips on, 182–183
   trotlines, 180
   using walking; stick for, 61
Flashlight, tracking and, 28
Folding walking stick, 52
Food
   growing. See Survival garden
   preservation methods for, 92–99
Footprint, aluminum foil, 106
Foraging, 7, 8
Fractures, first aid for, 116
Freeze-drying, as food preservation method, 95
Fresnel lens, 162
Friends, hiking with, 108–109
Frostbite, 121
Fuel, for fire, 158–159

G

Gardening, 66. See also Survival garden
Garlic, 72
   as medicinal plant, 13, 20–21
Gastrointestinal issues, first aid for, 118
Gatherings, bushcraft, 46–47
Getting lost, S.T.O.P. and, 113
Group tracking, 25
Gutters, for rainwater harvesting, 79, 80–82

H

Hammock, 44, 45
Harvested foods, preservation methods, 92–99
Hazardous situations
   adaptability to, 136
   mindset in, 126–137
Heat, for fire, 160–162
Heat exhaustion/stroke, 121
Heirloom seeds, 75
Help, universal signal for, 112
Herbal medicine. See Medicinal plants
Hiking
   basic gear for, 110–112, 124–125
   first-aid essentials, 114–125
   making known your route, 106
   preparation for, 104–112
Homesteading, 7, 8, 62–99. See also Rainwater catchment system; Survival garden
Hooks, for fishing, 178–179, 182
   trotlines and, 180
Hunting
   tracking and, 22–29
   using walking stick for, 61
Hygiene, for women, 44
Hypovolemic shock, 118

I

Ice packs, application of, 121
Insect bites, 118, 119
Instafire, 159
Itinerary, leaving in vehicle, 106

K

Kale, 72
Knife, 112, 140
   in fishing tackle, 182
   for survival shelter construction, 33
Knots, guide to tying, 164–175

L

Lanyards, breakaway, 140
Lean-to shelter, 33–35
Level of consciousness, 123
Line, fishing, 178
   trotlines, 180
Lost hiker, S.T.O.P. and, 113

M

Maps, 105, 140
Measuring tool, walking stick as, 57
Medicinal plants, 12–21
Mindset, in hazardous situations, 126–137
Mint, 13, 17
Motivational tools, in survival mindset, 137

N

Natural remedies. See Medicinal plants
Nausea and vomiting, 118
Neck, gear carried around, 140
Nettle, 13, 16
Notebook, 130

O

Oilcloth tarps
    how to make, 148–155
    for privacy, 44
Onions, 21
Online groups, bushcraft, 46
Oxygen, for fire, 162
Oxygen saturation, normal range, 123

P

Paracord bracelets, 140–141. See also Cordage
Parasitic infections, first aid for, 118
Paths, clearing with walking stick, 57
Peace of mind, preparation providing, 136
Peppers, 72
Pockets, organizing gear in
    backpacks and bags, 144
    clothing, 141
Positive thinking, 133, 136
Potatoes, 69
Preparedness, 7–8
Preservation methods,
    for harvested foods, 92–99
Pressure canners vs. pressure cookers, 98–99
Pressure dressing, 116
Prickly pear cactus, 13, 14, 17
Privacy, tarps for, 44
Psychology, in hazardous situations, 126–137
Pulse, normal range, 123
Pulse oximeter, 123

Purification methods. See Water disinfection; Water filter/filtration

R

Rainwater catchment system, 76–83
    estimating volume of, 78
    legalities of, 82
    preparing/maintaining, 78–82
    storage/treatment. See Water disinfection; Water filter/filtration
Reaching tool, walking stick as, 57
Research, on hiking conditions, 105, 107
Respiration, normal range, 123
Rewarming, 121
Rice, as desiccant, 90
R.I.C.E. formula, 118
Root cellars, for food storage, 94, 95–96
Rope. See Cordage

S

Safety tips. See also Survival planning
    walking stick as defense weapon, 61
    for women, 44
Seed vaults, 75
Seeds
    collecting/labeling, 88–89
    drying, 90–91
    heirloom, 75
    saving/storing, 86–87
    trading, 85
Self-reliance, 7, 8, 84–99
    bushcraft for, 10–61
    DIY projects, 146–183
    homesteading, 82–99
Shelters. See Survival shelters
Shoes/Boots, for women, 40
Sinkers, fishing, 179
Skin temperature/moisture, 123
Sleeping bags/pads, 44
Sling bags, 144
Smartwatch, vital signs and, 122, 123
Snakebites, 118
Solkoa Fastfire, 159
Space blanket. See Emergency blanket
Sphygmomanometer, 122
Splinting, 116
Sprains, first aid for, 116
Stethoscope, 122, 123

Stings. See Bites and stings
S.T.O.P. mnemonic, 113
Store-bought walking sticks, 52–53
Strains, first aid for, 116
Strangle knot, 172
Strength of will, 136
Strike-anywhere matches, 162
Sunflowers, 68
Superesse Straps, 141
Survival
    bushcraft for, 10–61
    planning for. See Survival planning
    psychology of, 126–137
Survival garden, 64–75
    crops for, 68–73
    establishing, tips on, 66, 74
    preserving harvest from, 92–99
    seed vaults for, 75
    seeds for. See Seeds
    surplus from, 69–70
Survival kit, 134–135
Survival planning, 8, 100–145
    first-aid essentials, 114–125
    precautionary measures, 102–112. See also Hiking
Survival shelters, 28–37
    locations to avoid, 33
    walking stick as support for, 56–57
Swivels, fishing, 179

T

Tarps. See Oilcloth tarps
Temperature, normal range, 123
Tinder
    heat sources for lighting, 160–163
    types of, 158–159
"Tinder tab" bundles, 159
Tomatoes, 73
Tools
    adaptations for women, 44
    motivational, in survival mindset, 137
    for survival shelter construction, 33
    used by tracker, 26
Tourniquet, 116
    improvised, 115
Track
    aerial signs, 26
    age of, 26
    features of, 26–27
    viewing perspectives, 24
"Track traps," 24

Tracking animals, 22–29
Tracking lost people, 106
Trail head, leaving itinerary details at, 106
Trail maps, 105, 140
Travel plans, communicating to others, 106
Trekking poles. See Walking sticks
Trotlines, 180
Tying knots, guide to, 164–175

U

USDA Plant Hardiness Zones, 68

V

Vehicle, leaving detailed itinerary in, 106
Vital signs, taking, 122

W

Walking sticks/staffs, 50–61
    sizing guidelines, 61
    types of, 52–53
    uses for, 52–61
Water
    checking depth of, 53, 58–59
    rainwater collection. See Rainwater catchment system
    in survival kit, 82
Water disinfection
    rainwater collection system, 77
    on trail/when hiking, 112, 118
Water filter/filtration
    rainwater collection system, 82
    on trail/when hiking, 112, 118
Wazoo Survival Gear, 140, 141
Weather conditions
    checking, 105, 107
    extreme, first-aid measures in, 121
Whistle, 111, 140
Wild medicinals. See Medicinal plants
Wilderness shelters. See Survival shelters
Wilderness survival, 10–61
Willow tree, 13, 16
Women, in the wilderness, 38–49
Wooden walking stick, 50–52
    tips on using, 53, 61
Wristwatch,
    vital signs and, 122, 123

PHOTO CREDITS

COVER Dzmitry Ryshchuk/Shutterstock; epicurean/E+/Getty Images **2-3** Hero Images/Getty Images **4-5** (Background) Jakub Krechowicz/Shutterstock (From left) Daxiao Productions/Shutterstock; Steve Atkins Photography/Alamy Stock Photo; Joshua Resnick/Shutterstock **6-7** Sophie Tempelhoff/EyeEm/Getty Images **8-9** Yifan Li/EyeEm/Getty Images **10-11** Presslab/Shutterstock **13** (Clockwise from top left) Christopher Nyerges; Evgenii Zotov/Getty Images; Tony Curry/Alamy Stock Photo; Christopher Nyerges; Rynovanderbijl93/Shutterstock; Christopher Nyerges **14** Rick Adams **16** (From left) azure1/Shutterstock; n_defender/Shutterstock **17** (From top) ©fitopardo.com/Getty Images; bonchan/Shutterstock **18-19** Sergi Escribano/Getty Images **20** Christopher Nyerges **21** lensblur/Getty Images **22-23** Mint Images - Art Wolfe/Getty Images **25** Hans Berggren/Getty Images **26-27** Craig Caudill **28-29** (From left) Hero Images Inc./Alamy Stock Photo; captureandcompose/Shutterstock **30-31** Paul Melling/Alamy Stock Photo **32** Oleksandr Rupeta/Alamy Stock Photo **33** (Clockwise from top) ShaunWilkinson/Shutterstock; Mega Pixel/Shutterstock; Craig Falls **34-35** Phoric/Shutterstock **36-37** Steve Atkins Photography/Alamy Stock Photo **38-39** Vlad Teodor/Shutterstock **40** Tracy Apperson **42-43** attilio pregnolato/Shutterstock **45** (Clockwise from top) Tracy Apperson; Ryan Rose; Tracy Apperson (2) **46-47** Hero Images/Getty Images **48-49** Kaitlyn McLachlan/500px/Getty Images **50-51** Tomas Rodriguez/Getty Images **52** (From left) NV Group Studio/Shutterstock; Peyker/Shutterstock; frantic00/Shutterstock **53** Henn Photography/Getty Images **54-55** Daxiao Productions/Shutterstock **56-57** sshepard/Getty Images **58-59** Dennis Tokarzewski/Shutterstock **60** Olga Koberidze/Shutterstock **62-63** Aliyev Alexei Sergeevich/Getty Images **64-67** Joshua Resnick/Shutterstock (2) **68-69** (Clockwise from top right) Drozdowski/Shutterstock; Jiang Hongyan/Shutterstock; Africa Studio/Shutterstock; Sommai/Shutterstock **70-71** cjp/Getty Images **72-73** (From left) Africa Studio/Shutterstock; Viktar Malyshchyts/Shutterstock; maxpro/Shutterstock; Antonova Ganna/Shutterstock; Tiger Images/Shutterstock; bergamont/Shutterstock; Jiang Hongyan/Shutterstock **74** Alexander Raths/Shutterstock **75** (From top) PeachLoveU/Shutterstock; Cattlaya Art/Shutterstock **76-77** Graphic.mooi/Shutterstock **79** Pack-Shot/Shutterstock **80-81** Radovan1/Shutterstock **83** jpr03/Alamy Stock Photo **84-85** Caron Badkin/Shutterstock **87** Temduang/Shutterstock **88-89** Jennylynn Fields/Shutterstock **90-91** ©fitopardo.com/Getty Images **92** Lawton, Becky/Getty Images **94** JRLPhotographer/Getty Images **96** JannHuizenga/Getty Images **97** B Brown/Shutterstock **98-99** NECHAPHAT/Shutterstock **100-101** Daxiao Productions/ Shutterstock **102-103** visionteller/Shutterstock **104-105** Everste/Getty Images **106** Dimitris Leonidas/Shutterstock **107** George jmclittle/Shutterstock **108-109** Tyler Olson/Shutterstock **110-111** Zheltyshev/Shutterstock **112** Ben Girardi/Aurora Photos/Getty Images **114** Lauzla/Getty Images **115** Vera Matejic **117** Presslab/Shutterstock **119** Vera Matejic **120-121** Daxiao Productions/Shutterstock **122** Blazej Lyjak/Shutterstock **123** (From top) suwatpatt/Shutterstock; John Kasawa/Shutterstock; kaitong.yepoon/Shutterstock **125** (From top) showcake/Shutterstock; Vera Matejic **126-127** Sven Zacek/Getty Images **128-129** deimagine/Getty Images **130-131** Hero Images/Getty Images **132-133** Jordan Siemens/Getty Images **134-135** Africa Studio/Shutterstock **137** (From top) Cavan Images/Getty Images; John Gollop/Alamy Stock Photo **138-139** Westend61/Getty Images **140** Eebenezer/Shutterstock **141** (From left) Olha Khomenko/Shutterstock; Carlos Joel/Shutterstock **142-143** Stock image/Shutterstock **144** S.Z./Shutterstock **145** Asmus Koefoed/Shutterstock **146-147** Veles-Studio/iStockPhoto **148** AVN Photo Lab/Shutterstock **149** Leon Werdinger/Alamy Stock Photo **150** AVN Photo Lab/Shutterstock **151** Todd Walker **152** Andrea Adlesic/EyeEm/Getty Images **153-155** Todd Walker (6) **156-157** slavemotion/Getty Images **159** nortongo/Shutterstock **160-161** Sue Wetjen/Shutterstock **163** Sjo/Getty Images **164-165** everst/Shutterstock **166-173** (Background) D M Smith Images/Shutterstock **166** Jonas Peschel/EyeEm/Getty Images **167** Michael D'Angona (4) **168** Adie Bush/Getty Images **169** Michael D'Angona (4) **170** Leon Harris/Getty Images **171-174** Michael D'Angona (18) **175** (From left) Olga Danylenko/Shutterstock; Ungor/Shutterstock **176-177** Rocksweeper/Shutterstock **179** MAHATHIR MOHD YASIN/Shutterstock **180-181** lightasafeather/Getty Images **182** Sergey Ash/Shutterstock **183** RubberBall Productions/Getty Images **184-185** Extreme-Photographer/Getty Images

---

The advice given in this book is the opinion of the author of each entry based on their personal experiences and knowledge. The right response to a disaster may not be the same in all situations. Articles are for informational purposes only. The publisher accepts no responsibility for injuries or liability arising from relying upon information contained herein. In the event of an emergency, follow the advice of first responders and trained professionals. Have a preparedness plan researched from multiple sources and avoid high-risk situations. Follow all applicable federal, state and local laws for firearm ownership, carry and usage.

SPECIAL THANKS TO CONTRIBUTING WRITERS
Tracy Apperson, Dane Boles, Craig Caudill, Michael D'Angona, Christopher Nyerges, Joshua Raines and Todd Walker

CENTENNIAL BOOKS

An Imprint of
Centennial Media, LLC
40 Worth St., 10th Floor
New York, NY 10013, U.S.A.

CENTENNIAL BOOKS is a trademark of Centennial Media, LLC

All rights reserved. No part of this publication may be reproduced, stored in a retrieval system, or transmitted in any form or by any means (including electronic, mechanical, photocopying, recording, or otherwise) without prior written permission from the publisher.

ISBN 978-1-951274-13-9

Distributed by
Simon & Schuster, Inc.
1230 Avenue of the Americas
New York, NY 10020, U.S.A.

For information about custom editions, special sales and premium and corporate purchases, please contact Centennial Media at contact@centennialmedia.com.

Manufactured in China

© 2020 by Centennial Media, LLC

Publishers & Co-Founders Ben Harris, Sebastian Raatz
Editorial Director Annabel Vered
Creative Director Jessica Power
Executive Editor Janet Giovanelli
Deputy Editor Alyssa Shaffer
Design Director Ben Margherita
Senior Art Director Laurene Chavez
Art Directors Natali Suasnavas, Joseph Ulatowski
Production Manager Paul Rodina
Production Assistant Alyssa Swiderski
Editorial Assistant Tiana Schippa
Sales & Marketing Jeremy Nurnberg